Propagate

Propagate

How to Regrow
Your Houseplants

Paul Anderton and Robin Daly
of **Two Dirty Boys**

Hardie Grant

BOOKS

Contents

Introduction

If you were to look down at Earth from space, you'd see a teeming mass of life forms in a complex network, competing for survival. From the bottom of the oceans to the hot, dry deserts, nature has found a way of persevering against the odds.

Unlike humans, plants have an astounding array of options when it comes to reproducing themselves. In simple terms, they can mate with other plants, get themselves pregnant, clone themselves or alter their cell function to grow roots and multiply. The mind boggles at their adaptability. It's no wonder plant life was here long before humankind came along, and it's not outrageous to think that they'll remain here long after we've exited the stage. It's this sense of magic that drove us to write this book. We're Paul and Robin, two friends who love growing things and we want to get people everywhere, just like us, propagating. We're not academics, we don't even know the Latin names for many of our plants, but each of the methods covered in the following pages has been tried and tested by us. The theory is that if we can do it, anyone can.

We know well the sense of achievement when you successfully propagate a plant, and nothing beats your first time. You'll take pride in generating a new independent organism, even though the skill was really mostly down to the plant itself.

So, join us on our journey into propagation as we explore different ways of multiplying plants. Nature offers us a marvellous mix of tools with which to generate new life.

With each of our propagation projects we grew more than we needed – and suggest you do too. They're the perfect gift – specially chosen, hand-nurtured and beautiful – to show how much you love and care.

What's more, propagating a plant is a wildly more sustainable alternative to buying a new one. In the UK, over 65 per cent of our houseplants are shipped in from the Netherlands where vast heated glasshouses mature the plants for sale. They are then transported hundreds of miles across Europe by road, adding more carbon to a shop-bought plant's already mucky footprint. This all becomes unnecessary when we harness the awesome power of propagation at home.

You'll notice that we've grouped the propagation projects into three sections according to difficulty, although, it should be noted that even those in the 'difficult' chapter are not particularly complex. As you work through the projects, we hope you'll be more confident and ambitious as you become familiar with the techniques and tips.

We met so many interesting people who helped us along the way. You'll find interviews with some of them dotted throughout the book. We found their stories fascinating and hope you do, too.

So, what are you waiting for? It's fun, it's fascinating, it's free and, most important of all, it's easy, so let's get propagating!

The Principles of Propagation

There are two main types of propagation and in both instances we are trying to fool the plant into thinking there is a natural process taking place.

Sexual propagation
This term is used to describe propagation from seeds and spores. This occurs through fertilisation and you'll see we explore this with a Peace lily, a Hart's tongue fern and an Echeveria succulent.

Asexual propagation
Plants don't need to be fertilised to generate new versions of themselves. Throughout the book we've tried to explore a wide variety of methods to do this. Broadly speaking they take the form of cuttings (leaves, plantlets, tips, stems or side shoots etc.), simple division of roots, or various types of layering – where the new plant remains partially attached to the mother plant while growing new roots.

Of course, in nature no plant is cut by a sterile knife, potted into a water-filled glass jar or placed in a plastic bag. Yet each of these stages mimics something that happens in nature. Plants have evolved to use damage, drought, their seeds being eaten – whatever it might be – to their advantage. In fact, these setbacks help them to spread, thereby increasing the species' chances of survival.

In the wild, nature can launch a million experiments in propagation every day, but you may have only a handful of cuttings, or perhaps as few as one very precious but poorly-looking stem. Therefore, when we propagate, we're aiming to increase our chances of success by hijacking the cutting's natural ability to regrow, and by putting it into near-perfect conditions.

Some plants propagate very easily. They're usually the vigorous kind, both in the wild and as houseplants. Coming from wet and warm tropical climates, where plants and animals compete for survival in nature's biological hothouse, these plants are used to being rained on torrentially and therefore forced to fight off waterborne infection. For that is the propagator's biggest enemy. The last thing anybody wants is for their cherished cutting to succumb to rot before it has a chance to lay down its roots. Much of each project's focus is preventing rot, and that's why you'll read many references to sterile equipment, so let's start there.

Sterilisation

Something is considered sterile when it has no bugs or germs living on its surface. A knife or jar can look spotlessly clean but be teeming with microscopic life. We use sterilisation to minimise the chance of these unwanted pests taking over your propagation project and killing your vulnerable fresh cutting. You can sterilise your equipment in three ways. Whichever method you choose, we don't recommend sterilising anything until shortly before you'll use it, otherwise airborne germs will undo all your good work.

1. Chemical sterilisation
Surgical spirit (known as rubbing alcohol in the USA) will kill all known germs dead, so it's a very effective steriliser. It'll kill your cutting, too, so it should be used only on your equipment and surfaces. Rub clean cotton buds (Q-tips), or paper towels, dipped in the alcohol over the surfaces you wish to sterilise, then leave to air-dry for a few minutes.

2. Warm soapy water
Many projects require little sterilisation beyond the knife blade. However, your equipment should be kept as clean and free of disease as possible, so for tools and equipment not specified, a careful wash (or a hot dishwasher programme) with warm soapy water should do the trick.

3. Temperature
Larger pieces of equipment and, especially, your growing medium, can't be sterilised with alcohol, so we tend to use the baking or boiling method for jars, lids, terracotta or ceramic pots and so on, and the baking method for potting mix.

To sterilise potting mix, place as much of it as you will need for your project into a deep baking tray (baking pan) and wet until damp all the way through. Then, cover it tightly with kitchen foil and bake in the oven. The length of time will depend on how much you are sterilising. You must make sure that the middle of the potting mixture has reached a sustained temperature of at least 72°C (160°F) – 15 minutes should be long enough. This will kill any bugs and germs. We've found that, as a general rule, 2kg (4lb 8oz) compost should be baked in the oven at 160°C (320°F, Gas 4) for 90 minutes.

Sterilise non-plastic items by pouring boiling water over them or using tongs to lower them into a pan of boiling water. A quick submersion in a rolling boil will sterilise anything heat-safe.

The propagator

Each project uses what is called a propagator, which is really just the term for the container that protects the cutting while it takes root. Some are as simple as a glass jar; other projects require a terrarium (we use a plastic storage crate), hermetically sealed (meaning airtight) from the outside world. The more complex propagator is designed to maintain a particular environment to increase the chances of the cutting taking root. Propagators create the ideal environment for the cutting, so they often inadvertently also make the perfect conditions for unwanted pests, bacteria and fungi. For this reason, the propagator should be kept as clean as possible, and a thorough sterilisation is a good place to start.

The growing medium

We've largely stuck to two types of growing medium for the projects in this book. You may have read about many more, and people do swear by a host of carefully tweaked and adapted recipes, but we have found that the most important characteristics of a growing medium are drainage and moisture retention. These differ in two main ways between propagations, depending on how moist the cutting likes its growing medium to be.

1. Tropical cuttings (that is to say, most houseplants) and plantlets – potting mix

These plants require a moist environment, as you find in the rainy, tropical habitats in which they evolved. Being naturally doused in heavy rain and then dried out by hot sun means they prefer a well-drained potting medium that holds some water. Five parts peat-free compost to two parts vermiculite (a natural mineral that both aerates the medium and retains water) is ideal.

2. Cacti and succulents – perlite mix
These plants need a mixture that is equal parts (50/50) peat-free compost and either gardeners' sand or perlite. This will ensure that any water is quickly drawn away from the developing succulents, mimicking the drought-with-occasional-rain pattern of watering they would receive in the wild.

It's worth noting that both these blends and a range of more specific growing media can be found at garden centres or online. Don't feel you're letting anybody down by not making your own – we often buy ours, and simply sterilise it at home as a precaution.

In addition, we've used coco coir (a by-product of the coconut industry) as a replacement for sphagnum moss, which isn't sustainably farmed. Coir is a fibrous material that is perfect, when wet, for the earliest stages of some plants' root propagation. As you'll see, once the roots have developed, the plants will need placing in potting mix, as coir is nutritionally poor.

Lastly, vermiculite plays an important role in a number of propagations as an additive to the potting mix. It can also be used on its own, as it is the ideal sterile rooting medium thanks to its invaluable water-retaining properties.

A quick note on language – we've avoided using the near ubiquitous word 'compost' as it is applied to many different growing media and can get confusing. The only time we'll use 'compost' is to describe shop-bought peat-free compost, just as you'd get from a garden centre, and regularly (but not always) labelled as compost. We use a general, good-quality peat-free compost. This is perfect for most propagations at the potting-on stage – once the cutting has rooted well and is ready to be potted on individually.

Hormone rooting powder

We've experimented with using and forgoing rooting powder as well as natural alternatives, such as honey or turmeric, and have found that nothing beats a good-quality bought powder. Some cuttings, such as monstera or purple heart, won't need it to take root, but, for those that do, it provides an essential boost and some antibacterial protection at a crucial stage in root development. We recommend decanting a small amount of the powder into a dish every time you use it, to avoid contaminating the original container with a dirty or infected cutting.

Water

Finally, we come to water and its essential role in propagation. Tap water is generally fine – we boil it and let it cool down completely – but we prefer to use rainwater. We live in London, where the water is drawn from below ground, which means it is full of minerals that can damage delicate baby plants or build up in the potting mix over time, causing problems. London can be surprisingly dry, so when there is enough rainwater about, and to prevent the chance of infection, we boil the collected rainwater in the microwave (it is not suitable for putting in your kettle) and leave it to cool.

When to propagate

It's always advisable to take cuttings in the spring or summer, during the growing phase (a few plants have their growing phase during the winter months, so, for those, take cuttings then). Take cuttings when the plant is at its most vibrant and likely to have the easily available energy (from the sun) needed to survive the trauma of being cut from its parent plant and growing a whole new vascular root system.

Always take a cutting from a healthy stem, one that is free of pests and disease and which looks vivid in colour. If the plant is not naturally so vibrant, the cutting should look like all the other shoots; don't choose the weak and sickly-looking straggler.

Aftercare

Houseplants are complex little creatures, forced to live in alien environments – such as your living room – thousands of miles from home. Every room is different, every pot, window or water type and weather pattern, so the variables that will affect how well your cutting thrives are numerous. Follow our tried-and-tested, step-by-step guide for each project and you should get a healthy propagation, but we do recommend researching each plant's specific aftercare thoroughly, since there is space on these pages for only a brief outline of what the plant will need into its adolescence and adulthood. Trial and error will ultimately be your guide, as you discover the personalities of each of your plant babies and where they are happiest in your home.

Easy

Propagate

Aspidistra

(Aspidistra elatior)

Root division

The aspidistra isn't called the 'cast-iron plant' for nothing – it is virtually indestructible (don't take that as a challenge). It was adored by the Victorians – who pretty much invented houseplants (see page 150) – and somehow seems to sum up the era, virtually gasping 'A handbag!' every time we brush past. If it's not Wildean quotations, then perhaps a few bars of 'The Biggest Aspidistra in the World'? This ludicrous music-hall ditty, made famous by Gracie Fields in the 1930s, tells the fantastical story of her brother who grows, you guessed it, the biggest aspidistra in the world. Fields re-recorded the song in 1941, adding the lines 'We will hang ol' Hitler from the very highest bough, of the biggest aspidistra in the world', and propagating a new wartime offshoot for her hammy music-hall hit. That same year, the British secret service bought the RCA radio transmitter from New York (then the largest in the world) and shipped it to England for use in the covert war effort. Its code name? 'Aspidistra', of course.

The aspidistra's sleek architectural lines, freed from the dark and chintzy interiors of our nineteenth-century forebears, make modern interiors pop. It is truly a plant for the ages. You can even use the leaves to serve food on, as they do in Japan, its original home. How about that?

Root division is a great way to propagate these plants. It's a very easy process, meaning you can multiply your aspidistra collection in no time. The secret of aspidistra propagation lies in their rhizomes, a kind of underground, modified stem that sends out offshoots and roots to form new plants. By dividing these up, you create entirely new aspidistra 'colonies'. Try to do it in the spring or early summer if possible, with the whole growing season ahead, to allow time for the new plants to establish before they fall dormant over the dark winter months.

You Will Need

— Newspaper, or some other kind of large
  paper covering, to collect the soil
— Sharp knife
— 3 or 4 pots, each roughly the same size
  as the original aspidistra pot
— Potting mix, enough to fill the pots

How to Propagate

Aspidistra

1 Spread out the paper and turn the potted aspidistra on its side. Ease the aspidistra – or rather, aspidistras (they are actually lots of plants in a clump) – out of the pot and on to the paper.

2 Tease the clump out into two, three or even four roughly equal-sized pieces, depending on its size. You'll need to get your hands in and work the clumps apart, judging by eye. Try not to break too many roots or the plant will have to spend time and energy recovering from the damage, instead of focusing on what it does best – growing gorgeous new foliage just for you. If you gently pull and work the roots apart, the clumps should soon come away.

3 You may need to cut through the crown (at the thickest part of the root ball) if it is really matted. Take a clean, sharp knife and make minimal cuts to separate the clumps. It might feel a bit barbaric, but remember, it's called the cast-iron plant.

4 Fill the pots with potting mix and pot up the divided clumps. Press them down just firmly enough to hold them upright and in place, and water generously.

Plant Care

Water	Aspidistra is very forgiving of a forgetful plant parent, being quite tolerant of drought. Ideally, it likes to be kept just moist over the summer months, and slightly drier in winter. You can allow the soil surface to become bone dry to the touch before you water. It is essential to use a free-draining growing medium, since aspidistras hate standing in water.
Food	As with most houseplants, feed only in summer. If anything, aspidistras enjoy less feeding than other houseplants, being so slow-growing.
Light	Aspidistra's range is epic! From bright (although mostly indirect) light through to a dark, gloomy corner, she can take it all. Robin's sits in the morning sun for an hour at dawn, before enjoying the relative gloom of his east-facing kitchen. Bright sunlight will scorch the leaves.
Temperature	This plant is well suited to cool conditions, and, like all houseplants, absolutely hates central heating.
Care	Aspidistras are low-maintenance and just like to be left to do their own thing, but don't leave them to gather dust. A wipe with a damp cloth every few days is a good idea to keep your plant (Robin's is called Oscar) looking resplendent.
Also try this with	Peace lily, philodendron and asparagus fern

Chain of Hearts

(Ceropegia)
Butterfly propagation

This is one of our favourite houseplants, being essentially indestructible and so easy to propagate. Paul's grows next to his shower, creating the vibe of a tropical waterfall fringed with exotic foliage. Coming from South Africa, the chain of hearts loves warmth and humidity, making the bathroom an ideal choice. It must never stand in water, however, and should be watered only when the soil is dry. Paul occasionally splashes his and adds a palmful or two of warm – but not soapy – water when it needs it.

The butterfly propagation technique is beautifully simple. The long strings, or chains, of hearts will grow to huge lengths if the plant is happy and left to its own devices. If you cut them off, the chain will regrow from the cut on the mother plant, so, don't worry about harvesting cuttings from a mature specimen.

You Will Need

- Plastic container to put your cuttings in (they are compact cuttings, so a small container can accommodate a surprisingly large number)
- Coco coir (soaked in water for an hour and wrung out tightly using clean hands), enough to fill the container to a depth of 3–4cm (1¼–1½in)
- Potting mix
- Sharp knife or scissors
- Cling film (plastic wrap) or plastic bag (optional)

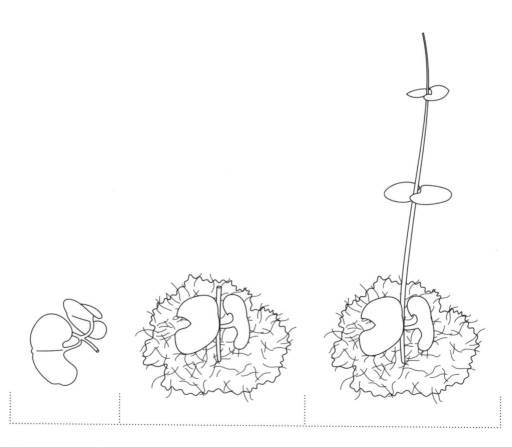

How to Propagate

Chain of Hearts

1 First, prepare the propagation dish by filling it with about 3–4cm (1¼–1½in) of coir. We use a plastic container, but you might choose something more decorative if you are propagating on a mantelpiece or windowsill (see step 8 for a tip on the size of your dish). Don't scrimp on the coir: it has to be this depth to retain enough moisture to encourage the roots to form. Press it down so it's compacted, and use a water spray to wet it thoroughly, but not so much that water pools at the bottom.

2 Cut the chains into individual pairs of hearts, removing the excess 'string' to about 1cm (½in) each side of the paired hearts.

3 Gently push one end of each cut 'string' into the coir and repeat until all your cuttings, or as many as will fit into the container, are secure. It doesn't matter which end you push in; this is just to secure the cutting. Leave a little space between the cuttings – they shouldn't touch, since if one fails and rots, the rot will spread if they are too closely packed.

4 Spray the cuttings with water and leave to root. You'll need to make sure the containers don't dry out, so check them daily. We have tried wrapping the dish in cling film or a plastic bag, which means you will need to water only about once a week, but, if you do this, you must be extra-vigilant and remove any cuttings that die – as some will – before they rot in the humidity under the plastic. The mould will spread and, if unchecked, could wipe out the whole batch.

5 Make a small hole in the cling film, if using, as a good compromise between ensuring moisture retention and allowing air circulation to prevent rot.

6 Once your cuttings are established, you'll see new little chains that reach out vertically and then tumble over the edge of the dish. If using a plastic bag or cling film, you should remove it once the shoots emerge.

7 Pot your cuttings on once two or three butterfly leaves have formed. By this time the roots will have mingled with the coir and, although they are fairly robust, be careful when removing them not to cause damage. Tease them out gently by hand.

8 If you have a pot in mind for your new chain of hearts plant, you can specifically choose a propagation dish that is of the same dimensions as that final pot. That way, when it comes to potting on, you can simply transfer the mat of coir and cuttings to the new pot, where it will happily bed in once filled with potting mix. If not, then cut the mat accordingly, or tease out the baby plants and bury the roots gently in the potting mix.

Plant Care

Water	Chain of hearts needs to dry out between waterings, so be sparing.
Food	Once a month, over the summer months, your chains will thank you for a light feed of a balanced liquid houseplant fertiliser.
Light	Chain of hearts is very tolerant. Even though it loves indirect bright light, it'll survive with something a little more gloomy if need be.
Note	Sometimes, chain of hearts becomes all chain and no hearts. Perhaps a house-sitter overwatered while you were away? Don't be afraid to cut them back, since they'll happily resprout from the nodes below the trim (i.e. towards the root). If this is your first time, perhaps cut just a few of the chains and watch them regrow, to calm your nerves.

Propagate

Monstera

(Monstera deliciosa)

Mid-stem cutting

The most gloriously camp plant that ever lived, this one can grow into a real monster, just as the name suggests. Monstera has been a firm favourite since the 1970s, but with none of the unsavoury undertones of the pampas grass.

The reason for its Latin genus name, *Monstera*, is lost in the mists of time, but it could refer to the huge size of the plant, or the strange shape of the leaves. In the tropical forests of Central America, a monstera can grow to over 20m (65ft) tall, using the aerial roots you'll recognise from your own houseplant to climb up through the tree canopy. The second part of the name, *deliciosa*, refers to the fruit, which was farmed in the nineteenth century and is said to taste like a cross between pineapple and banana. We've never had even a hint of a fruit on ours, but then London isn't known for its domestic tropical-fruit industry.

It is possible to take so many cuttings from one monstera that, if you're willing to cannibalise your pride and joy, you could propagate tens of new plants from a large one. Large or leggy (growing long stems with few or no leaves), monstera is ideal for taking cuttings from.

You Will Need

— Pot large enough to accommodate the cutting
— Potting mix
— Sharp knife
— Cane and string (optional)

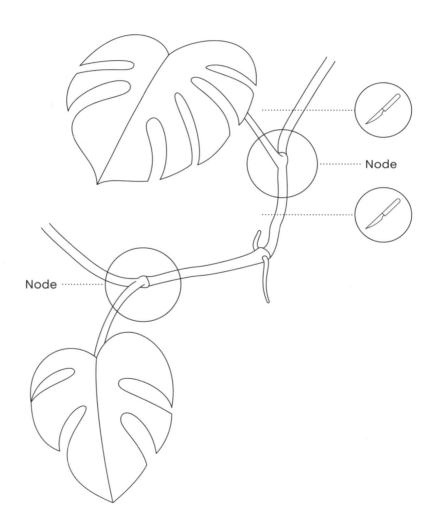

Node

Node

How to Propagate

Monstera

1   Each plant is different, so in order to understand where to make the cuts, you need to inspect the stems carefully. It doesn't matter if your plant is leggy; the most important thing is to identify the nodes. Nodes are the ridges on the stems where leaves are or used to be attached. If you can, choose a section of stem that looks healthy, with large, waxy leaves that are firm, not limp. If you are propagating because your monstera is dying, give it a go anyway. It's worth a try, just find the best stem you can.

2   Prepare the pot by filling it with potting mix and firming the surface.

3   Make the first cut about 5cm (2in) above a node (i.e. away from the roots). You can even use the tip of the stem if you are making only one cutting.

4   If you are making more than one cutting, next make a second cut just below the next node down (i.e. towards the roots). This will give you two cuttings, the end – or terminal – cutting, and a mid-stem cutting below it. The length of your cuttings will depend on the distance between nodes. If the nodes are close together, you may include more than one in your cutting. The most important thing is that you have at least one node in each cutting. Ideally, at least one of the nodes in your cutting will have a leaf. This will increase the chance of the cutting 'taking' (rooting).

5 Monstera roots from the node, not from the cut, so you don't need to dip the cutting in hormone rooting powder. If the cutting has leaves, it is easy to tell which way up to plant it but, if it's leafless, pay extra attention to the cutting's natural top and bottom from the start so you don't get mixed up. Lay the stem flat on the surface of the potting mix and press it down to bury the cutting, leaving the leaf stem (or petiole) above the surface. If the leaves are large they may pull the cutting over, or out of the potting mix entirely. If that happens, use a cane pushed into the potting mix as a support, and attach one of the leaves with string to keep the cutting upright. Ideally, you'll take a cutting with two or three leaves, but monstera is so vigorous that it will try to root with no leaves. It is less likely to succeed, though, so use this method only in emergencies.

6 The first leaves that emerge from the new plant will be small, and won't have the characteristic holes in the leaves. This is a perfectly normal part of the plant's development. The larger, holey leaves will form over the coming months.

Tip

Monstera can also be propagated by placing the stem cutting in water in a high-sided glass jar or other container for a few weeks. The best thing about starting it off in water is that you can see when the roots develop. This method is quicker than rooting in potting mix, too. However, there are a couple of things to bear in mind:

• You'll need to change the water regularly, perhaps twice a week.

• If the cutting has spent a long time rooting in water, the roots it produces will be specially designed aquatic roots. If you want to pot it on into soil, trim the roots to about 2cm (¾in) long and leave the cutting in water for a couple more weeks, to grow new roots, until they are about 2cm (¾in) long too. These new roots won't be specialised yet, and so will be able to adapt to work in soil.

Plant Care

Water	You'll need to water your plant every two weeks in the summer (every week in a hot spell), but during the winter perhaps only once a month (depending on how high you have your central heating). Water only when the top few centimetres (an inch) of the potting medium is bone dry. Try to use rainwater or filtered water, especially if you live in an area of hard water. Monstera loves humidity, but can tolerate the dryness of most indoor habitats well. If you mist it once in a while and wipe its leaves with a damp cloth to clean off dust, it'll love you forever.
Food	Feed a monstera each month during the growing season using an all-purpose liquid fertiliser. Also, make sure you feed your plant directly after it's been repotted, as it will need extra nutrients during this period of stress and new growth.
Light	Monstera loves light, but it shouldn't be direct. If you bought your plant new it will probably have been acclimatised to indirect light as most commercial houseplants come from these kind of settings, but it's possible to introduce your monstera slowly to a little more direct light over time.
Note	The leaves and stems of monstera can irritate the skin and eyes, as can the fruit if it's not ripe. Make sure you wash your hands with soap and water after handling these cuttings. In the unlikely event that you get your plant to fruit, apparently you must wait until the outer scales drop off before you eat it. Good luck!
Also try this with	Corn plant (*Dracaena*), golden pothos (*Epipremnum aureum*) and prayer plant (*Maranta*)

Propagate

Spider Plant
(Chlorophytum comosum)

Runners

The spider plant is the rookie propagator's entry-level, sweet-spot starter plant, since it can be propagated in not one, but two of the easiest ways. The plantlets that grow from runners, sent out by the parent plant, are called spiderettes, and are essentially propagating themselves.

Strictly speaking, this isn't a mother-and-baby situation, and has more in common with Dolly the Sheep, as these spiderettes are in fact clones. (In 1996, this famous – or infamous – Scottish sheep was the first animal in the world to be cloned, that is, made from the genetic material of only one parent, making it an exact copy.) Each spiderette is similarly genetically identical to the parent plant. When a spider plant is mature and happy, it will send out offshoots that flower. These flowers, if left unfertilised, will develop into a tiny spider plant, making a break for a new life far(ish) from home.

Not long after Robin first moved to London, around the turn of the millennium, when fears of the Y2K bug were all anybody talked about, he moved to Broadway Market in Hackney. Despite its name, the market didn't really exist beyond a handful of struggling shops and a woman who seemed to sell nothing but baby spider plants from the boot (trunk) of a knackered old Volvo estate. Her business model was terrible, though, as we haven't had to buy a new spider plant since, simply propagating from that one original spiderette from more than 20 years ago.

You Will Need

— If rooting in potting mix: plant pots (10cm/4in diameter is ideal), potting mix and paperclips
— If rooting in water: glasses or glass jars, and marbles/pebbles (optional)
— Scissors, secateurs or sharp knife

How to Propagate

Spider Plant

1   When the spider plant is mature, it will start to send out offshoots that look like stalks and have flowers at the end. Once the spiderettes start to form, place the mother plant in the middle of a table or on the floor, since you need an area large enough for the spiderettes and their pots.

2   To grow in potting mix, count the spiderettes and fill the same number of small pots with potting mix. Surround the mother plant with the pots, then take a spiderette and match it to a pot, positioning the pot so that the spiderette's running stem is not twisted or taut. Once you've found the natural place for the pot, simply press the spiderette into the potting mix and hold it down with an opened-out paperclip, to give the spiderette the best chance of taking root.

3   The process is similar with water: just replace the pots with glasses or jars of water. Don't fill them too deep, since you only want to cover the developing roots. You can use marbles or pebbles to hold the spiderette in place, with just the base of the spiderette touching the surface of the water. The water level will fall as the plant drinks, and through evaporation, so you will need to keep topping it up.

4

Over several weeks you will begin to notice your spiderettes have developed their own roots, either in the soil or in water. Simply take a pair of scissors or secateurs, or a sharp knife, and snip the spiderette away from the main plant where the long stem meets the spiderette. Transfer them to potting mix and a suitably sized pot, so they can continue to grow into a strong and healthy spider plant.

Tips

If you prefer, you can just as easily cut the spiderettes free of the mother plant as they dangle in mid-air. Try to wait until the spiderette has developed some little trailing air roots underneath it, then cut it off and pot it up or place it in water to root.

Spider plants do tend to get pot-bound (when the roots crowd the pot and stunt the growth and vitality of the plant), so you should aim to repot into a larger pot, or divide them (see aspidistra project, page 19), every couple of years.

Plant Care

Water	Spider plants are a bit of a Goldilocks when it comes to water, so little and often is ideal as they need it to be 'just right'. They are fairly forgiving, though; just try not to let them dry out.
Food	Give a general houseplant feed in the spring and summer from the second year onwards; in the first year, they should have plenty of nutrients from the new potting mix you have used to plant them up in.
Light	It is often said that spider plants should be grown in indirect light, but a little direct light shouldn't be a problem, especially if you have a variegated type, which needs extra light to photosynthesise. Experiment with your new plants – you'll probably have so many that if you really want to try one in the sun, you can give it a go. You'll know if it's not happy: the leaf tips will turn brown.
Temperature	Spider plants can grow outside in the summer in milder areas, and can tolerate a wide range of temperatures, and humidity.

Propagate

Bunny-ear Cactus

(Opuntia microdasys)

Pad cutting

Paul's first experience of propagating a cactus came during a house move. It's inevitable that houseplants will take a few knocks on moving day, but this ever-so-patient bunny-ear cactus got crushed by a poorly placed microwave oven and snapped into three pieces.

The great news is that cactus plants are happy being broken into bits and grown as individual plants; in fact, they produce offsets, or pups (baby versions of themselves), naturally. There's no magic propagation technique, but the conditions needed for the new plants to prosper can be a challenge if you happen to be an 'over-carer'. Cacti are desert plants, which means they are sensitive to overwatering. In its natural habitat a cactus might sit around sunning itself for months on end before it gets its share of rainfall, so it's become an expert at hoarding water when it finally gets the chance. You might expect a thirsty plant like this to grow deep roots, but their root systems are shallow and wide to absorb lots of surface water before the hot sun returns and evaporates the rainfall.

Take care not to touch the fine spines with your bare hands. This plant may share a name with a soft and fluffy bunny, but the similarities end there.

The following propagation technique works well for a range of cacti, as long as you do it in early summer rather than over the winter. We've had success at home with tree cactus, pineapple cactus and the desert candle.

You Will Need

— Gardening gloves
— Gardening scissors or pruning knife
— Small clay or terracotta pot
— Pebbles or rocks, for draining
— Perlite mix

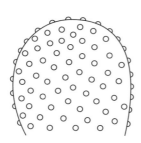

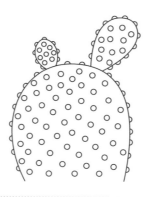

How to Propagate

Bunny-ear Cactus

1 — Wearing gardening gloves, snap away or use scissors or a knife to prune off a section of 'bunny ear'. This cutting will become your new baby cactus.

2 — Leave the cutting to dry on a clean, sunny windowsill until the wound has become callused and dry (about 48 hours).

3 — Fill the plant pot a quarter full with pebbles or small rocks.

4 — Now fill the pot to the top with perlite mix.

5 — Plant the cutting into the pot, pushing it 2–4cm (¾–1½in) into the perlite mix. If your cutting is top-heavy and won't stand up on its own, you can lie it lengthways in the soil.

6 — Position the pot in a sunny and dry environment, watering sparingly but regularly. You'll know the cutting has taken root when it continues to grow and eventually produces its own pups.

Propagate

Plant Care

Water	Remember that cacti are sensitive to too much water, which can lead to root rot. During the summer and in a warm room you may water the plant once every week or two, but make sure the perlite mix is allowed to dry out between waterings. If you are using a drip tray, make sure there's no standing water present. Over the winter, as the plant becomes dormant, watering once a month or less will be adequate.
Food	Feed with cactus plant food once a year in the spring or early summer.
Light	Although cacti love the sun, they can still suffer from sunburn if the sun is too direct and persistent, so pick a location that receives at least a little shade at some point during the day.
Temperature	As you might expect, cacti like it warm over the summer months, but remember to keep them in a cooler environment over winter, when they are dormant.
Also try this with	Thimble cacti (*Mammillaria gracilis*) or Easter lily cactus (*Echinopsis subdenudata*)

Plants, Pots and Personalities

Most guides to propagation take a utilitarian approach when it comes to selecting growing apparatus and pots. We met with the Hackney, East London-based ceramic artist Alex Smith (@alexsmithceramics) to learn why propagation vessels needn't be joyless.

You're an illustrator, animator and ceramicist. Where does propagation fit into all that?
I spend long periods either at my desk or in the studio, so I'm stuck in the same place for hours on end. I've worked out that propagating cuttings and surrounding myself with all these mini plants brings some amazing energy into my workspace. I like to enhance the personalities of my plants by creating vessels and pots that match their mood. Plants have their own dispositions, and this is something you can really play around with to enhance the mood of a desktop.

We love to play around with outer pots for houseplants. You can change the mood of your living room in minutes. How do you use mood and personality in your work?
Many of the growing pots or vases I create quite literally have faces on them. So, I can match up a slow-growing cactus with the face of a sleepy old man, or the frantic energy of a tomato cutting with a suitable psychotic expression. These personalities fill up my studio. Now I'm never alone!

I'm sure, just like us, you find propagation surreal. After all, you're generating a new living organism. How do you capture that idea in your ceramics?
There's something dreamlike about propagation that inspires me. One of my favourite recent pottery pieces is called 'the grow-worker'. It's a little ceramic character that sits on the side of a cup of water and doubles as a self-watering pot for a seedling. It's like a little piece of art that's on the move. Every day it's grown and changed a little bit – I just love the way the object interacts with nature. It's a great way to celebrate a new seedling or cutting.

We considered all sorts of plants to propagate before we began research on this book, but you've started growing something poisonous, haven't you? Tell us why on Earth you're growing your own deadly nightshade.
Morbid curiosity, really. I first heard of *Atropa belladonna* when I was studying film. They said that early Hollywood starlets would use the plant to dilate their pupils so as to draw the viewers further into their sultry gaze. Deadly nightshade is poisonous to humans and animals, so I'm being extremely careful – and I'm growing some black tomatoes that are part of the same family, so I've taken extra measures not to get them mixed up.

Propagate

Cordon Tomato Plants

(Solanum lycopersicum)

Propagation from side shoots

Each year we grow tomatoes on the allotment, and each year we fight with each other about what we're doing wrong. It's not that we don't get a tomato crop, it's just that it doesn't ever live up to the technicolour beauty contest of heirloom sex bombs filling our Instagram feed throughout the late summer. It appears that six-year-olds across the world can grow better tomatoes than us without even trying.

However, when our tomatoes have worked, they've all arrived at once, yielding armfuls of sun-ripened fruit over a short period. We've picked them, sun-dried them and given them to neighbours to get the most out of the sudden glut. Propagating a tomato plant as it grows is a great way of staggering your harvest, allowing you to have a number of plants maturing at different times over the summer.

The leggy and energy-packed cordon tomato plant isn't the prettiest of shapes. Over the growing season its eager side shoots burst out in all directions in a riot of explosive energy. These should be removed whether or not you'll be propagating, because they can inhibit the production of fruit by diverting energy into excessive leaf production. And it's these little shoots that hold the key to easy propagation. Think of them as little seedlings wanting to break free of their overbearing mother plant.

You Will Need

— Secateurs
— Glass of fresh, clean water
— Small plant pot
— Potting mix

How to Propagate

Cordon Tomato Plants

1 On an established mother plant that is producing unneeded side shoots, select a healthy shoot that is around 10cm (4in) long and free of pests or blight. Cut it off using secateurs.

2 If the shoot has several leaves, remove the lower ones to reveal a clean, straight stem.

3 Place the stem in the glass of water and position the vessel in a bright and warm environment, out of direct sunlight. We usually choose a kitchen windowsill so that we can keep an eye on the cutting as it grows.

4 Refresh the water each day, refilling the glass so that the stem is submerged but the leaves stay dry. Within a week or two the cutting will have grown its own healthy root system and be ready for planting out.

5 Once you're happy with the look of the new roots, fill the small plant pot with potting mix and use your finger to make a hole just big enough for the cutting. Place the roots of the cutting in the potting mix and gently firm it in with your fingers.

6 Water the new tomato plant, place the pot in a bright, warm and preferably humid spot, and watch the cloned plant grow.

Propagate

Plant Care

Water	Tomatoes require a large amount of water, especially if they are growing in pots. They mustn't dry out, which means watering your plants anything from twice a day to once a week. Keep an eye on them for wilting or dry roots and learn how much your tomato plant needs.
Food	Once flowers appear on your tomato, you can feed the plant weekly with liquid tomato food. At this point, you can also remove some of the leaves sheltering the flowers, to give more light to the emerging fruit.
Light	Tomatoes love a sunny but sheltered spot such as a bright greenhouse. They enjoy some direct sun, but too much can cause sunburn.
Temperature	Tomatoes love warmth, and thrive in polytunnels and behind glass
Also try this with	Try growing tomatoes with basil, which enjoy the same conditions and tastes great when combined. You can propagate basil in the same way as tomato shoots. Both are best eaten directly from the plant on a warm summer evening.

Propagate

Jade Plant

(Crassula ovata)
Leaf cutting

Some say there's no magic money tree, but they're categorically wrong. The jade plant also goes by the names lucky plant, money plant and, sometimes, money tree. It originated in the warm climate of South Africa and Mozambique, but now it's found in homes all over the world, not least because it's so easy to grow. The level of care needed is emphatically low; it doesn't need much watering and can sit quietly in the corner, pretty stress-free, for weeks on end. With a tiny bit of care and attention a jade plant will even outlive you, since many live for more than 100 years.

In the wild, the jade plant's main method of reproduction – as with many other succulents – is vegetative propagation, whereby its leaves, or even branches, fall off and take root close by. This means it's an exceptionally easy propagator.

Some believe the jade plant brings good luck, financial gain and prosperity. In our experience, it tends to bring with it little pests called mealybugs. If you've got these stowaways, you'll know it when you see fluffy white patches on the plant's stems. These bugs also poop out a sweet, sticky substance called honeydew, which acts as a starter home to fungal diseases. If, like us, you are unfortunate enough to have discovered a mealybug infestation a simple 50/50 mix of apple cider vinegar and water applied to the affected area through a spray bottle should do the trick. Don't let all this put you off, though; the jade plant is a piece of cake to grow. If your jade is particularly happy with its conditions, it'll flower over the winter with a sweetly scented bloom.

You Will Need

— Paper towel
— Small plant pot
— Perlite mix

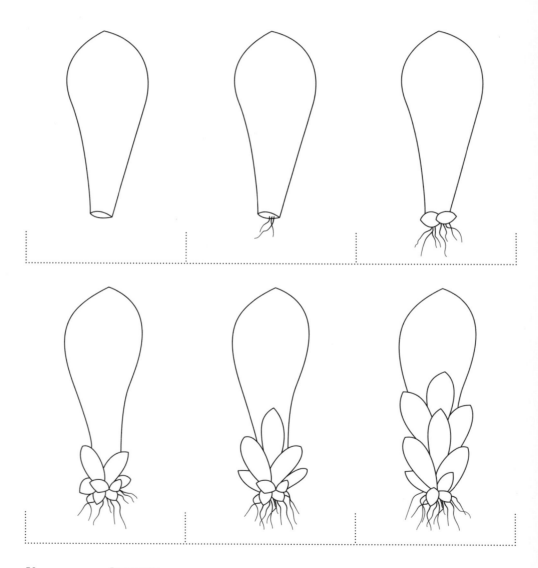

How to Propagate

Jade Plant

1 Start by choosing the healthiest leaf you can find and plucking it from the stem (choose a large, plump one that's free from marks or bruising).

2 Put the leaf on a clean dry surface, such as a paper towel, and leave it for a day or two in a dry place, such as on a sunny windowsill, so that the wound dries out and becomes callused.

3 Fill the small pot with perlite mix and water sparingly. Make sure the pot is draining properly – jade plants hate it wet.

4 Place the leaf on top of the perlite mix in the new pot, and leave in a bright place. Water it regularly so that the perlite mix does not dry out.

5 After about four weeks, roots will begin to form on the severed leaf. These will look like fine hairs at first, so be sure not to disturb their descent into the perlite mix by knocking or moving the cutting. Tiny, bubble-like foliage will appear soon after the new roots have formed.

6 After several more weeks, you'll have a separate jade plant growing from your jade leaf. At this point, it's big enough to pot on.

Propagate

Plant Care

Water	It's tempting to overwater a jade plant when you're doing the weekly watering rounds, but too much water can cause both leaf drop and root rot.
Food	Add some succulent plant food monthly when watering over the summer.
Light	Lots of light is best for the jade plant.
Temperature	This is a plant that grows well at room temperature in a dry environment.
Also try this with	*Kalanchoe blossfeldiana* 'Don Nando'

Propagate

Chinese Money Plant

(Pilea peperomioides)

Plantlets

It's astounding to think that the first known published image of a Chinese money plant was in *Kew Magazine* in 1984. Here we have a great example of a plant that found its way across the world through networks of amateur gardeners before it was recognised by botanists as noteworthy.

Although popular in China as a token of good luck, this plant had such a mysterious journey to Europe that, in 1983, *The Sunday Telegraph* published an article asking the public to contact the Royal Botanic Garden at Kew if they could help solve the puzzle of its arrival in the United Kingdom. One family were able to help, tracing their propagated plant back via a gift from a Norwegian *au pair*.

The story caught the imagination of Dr Lars Kers of the Botanic Garden in Stockholm, who brought the plant on to a popular Swedish TV programme to show the public. The resulting onslaught of enquiries and letters eventually laid the mystery bare. In 1945, a Scandinavian missionary named Agnar Espegren had taken a cutting home with him when fleeing Hunan province in China at the end of World War II. He propagated the plant and passed it among his friends. For this reason, the Chinese money plant is also known as the missionary plant!

You can take stem cuttings to propagate this plant, but there's not much reason to do so. Just keep it happy and it'll propagate itself, producing baby versions in abundance.

You Will Need

— Small plant pot
— Potting mix
— Sharp knife

How to Propagate

Chinese Money Plant

1   A few weeks before you want to propagate it, move your adult Chinese money plant into a brighter spot than usual (but not in direct sun) and pay closer attention to its watering regime. The aim is to give your plant the optimum levels of light and water to kick-start its propagation.

2   You should notice little plantlets appearing at the base of the plant. Let these grow until each has several fully formed leaves.

3   When you're ready to propagate, fill the small pot with potting mix. Using the knife, slice a plantlet away from the base of the stem.

4   Plant the baby plant into the new pot and water immediately. Keep the potting mix moist over the coming weeks as the plant establishes its root system.

Plant Care

Water	Water approximately once a week. Take care not to overwater, or leave the plant in standing water, or it will quickly lose its leaves.
Food	Feed the plant once a month over the spring and summer.
Light	Chinese money plants like light, so keep them somewhere bright but out of direct sunlight.
Temperature	These plants operate best at room temperature, and must not get cold. Avoid allowing their environment to drop below 10°C (50°F).
Also try this with	Banana plant (*Musa velutina* – only the *Musa* variety will produce plantlets) and vriesea

How Plants Connect People

Munir Malik is a director and writer with a propagation fixation. We asked him why his favourite houseplant is the purple heart?

Tell us why purple heart is so close to your heart.

I first discovered this plant when I drove Anna-Maria, my dearest friend and flatmate of nine years, back home to Cologne. It was cascading over a balcony at her brother's family home and I couldn't help but take a cutting home with me as a memento. It's become a reminder of our ongoing friendship.

The great thing is it's so easy to propagate. The stems are visibly segmented, so I just snip a piece off and leave it in water for a couple of weeks and roots emerge at the joints.

When we propagate, we sometimes get carried away and end up with more than we bargained for. Do you have the same problem with purple heart?

I can't get enough of it. In its natural habitat in Mexico, the purple heart sort of scrambles across the earth, so when it's grown as a houseplant it tends to get leggy. Propagation is a great way of adjusting the shape by cloning lots of baby versions and sticking them back into the main pot to create a more rounded shape.

The other reason I can never have too many multiples of this plant is that it makes a brilliant gift for friends. I've moved house more than I'd like to mention over the last few years, and I always seem to leave behind a purple heart plant. There's literally a trail of living specimens across Europe because of my handiwork.

Do you have any tips for keeping purple heart at its best?

It's easy to take care of and very fast-growing – I mean, in the growing season you can almost see it creeping across your living room. It is tolerant of drought so it thrives on neglect, but it is also happy being watered weekly, so you can't go wrong.

I've noticed that purple heart is at its most vibrant when it gets full sun. In shadier environments the leaves can turn pale green.

I've also had a few accidents whereby the plant grows so long and heavy on one side that it topples from the shelf. Since then, I've made sure I use a heavy and well-balanced outer pot, so we don't have any nasty surprises.

We read that purple heart is great at improving indoor air quality by filtering volatile organic compounds (pollutants and irritants). Is this part of the reason you're such a big fan?

Yes definitely – and these plants are great for spaces that have problems with damp because they help in regulating the moisture in the air! Oh, and one more thing to look out for is its beautiful, delicate pink flowers each spring. They're really very pretty.

Medium

Propagate

African Violet

(Streptocarpus sect)
Leaf (petiole) cutting

The Two Dirty Boys love a bit of camp. The spirit of extravagance seems to be the very definition of plants, and it is part of the reason we love them so much. Many display a definite bent towards the fabulous and flamboyant, while others, such as the African violet, embrace a different sort of camp, one that is less fashionable but just as wonderful. You could call it an English camp of matching tea sets, silk scarves, wry smiles and working-men's clubs, where an African violet was often found as a table decoration, next to a full ashtray. In recent years, this plant has gained new admirers, perhaps as the wheel of fashion turns once more or perhaps as a deliberate nod to this beautiful plant's *déclassé* past.

African violets are the perfect specimen to try your hand at leaf cuttings. This variation of the method is for plants with a petiole, the scientific name for the stalk that attaches the leaf to the plant stem.

You Will Need

— Plant pot large enough to accommodate the leaf
— Potting mix
— Sharp knife
— Clear plastic bag wide enough to fit over the pot
— Elastic band or string

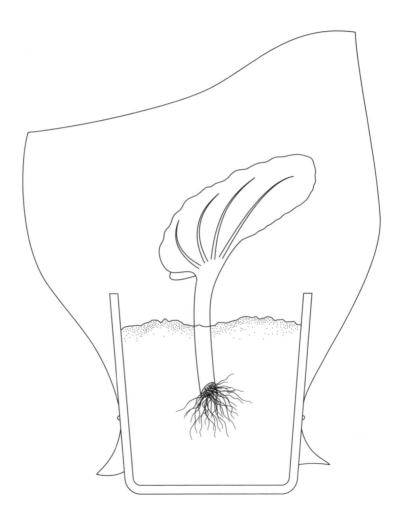

How to Propagate
African Violet

1 — First, prepare the pot by filling it with potting mix and firming the surface.

2 — Choose leaves that are almost fully grown. These will be at their fastest pace of growth, while also being developed enough to survive the trauma of being amputated from the parent plant. Cut off your chosen leaf and up to 4cm (1½in) of petiole, making a clean, crisp cut with no ragged edge.

3 — Pop the lower end of the stalk into the potting mix, deep enough that the leaf blade is held upright. Gently firm around it so that it stays in place.

4 — To keep the cutting warm, moist and free of disease as it roots, place a clear plastic bag over it and secure it with an elastic band or piece of string. Now watch for a new plant growing from where the petiole is buried.

5 The new plants should begin to form in four or five weeks, at which point you can remove the bag and let them grow on until they're large enough to pot up individually. It can take up to two months to reach this stage, though, so be patient.

6 It's hard to tell if the leaves have rooted, so we'd recommend propagating more than you need so that you can sacrifice some after a month by digging them up and checking if roots are forming. You might be tempted to perform a 'tug test' to see if the roots have emerged, but you are likely to damage the fine new roots if you do. If the other leaves still look healthy, you can assume they've all taken root to the same stage.

Tips

In theory, you can do this all year round, but it's invariably less successful in deepest winter, unless you have a propagator with artificial light and heat.

Large plants can also be divided, by cutting the parent plant into sections or trimming off and potting on any suckers. But we think leaf-cutting propagation is more fun and more than a little bit magical.

Plant Care

Water	African violets are very sensitive to cold water, so always use room-temperature water when watering, and avoid getting any on the leaves. They do, however, need a humid environment, and for the best results you should stand the pot on a tray of gravel half-filled with water. Once the soil surface is dry to touch, water the plants by placing them in trays of water for 30 minutes, allowing their soil to soak up new moisture.
Food	To ensure brightly coloured blooms, use a houseplant food monthly, adding this in liquid form to the reservoir of water in the watering trays.
Light	Even though African violets originally hail from Africa, as their name suggests (Tanzania and tropical coastal Kenya, to be precise), they're surprisingly hardy as houseplants and love diffused bright light during spring and summer. Once winter sets in, however, you're best advised to move your African violet to a south-facing windowsill (north-facing in the southern hemisphere) if possible. Just make sure to keep it out of draughts at all times.
Also try this with	*Hoya* and *Peperomia*

Heart-leaf Philodendron

(Philodendron)

Compound layering

'Philodendron' comes from the ancient Greek word *philo*, meaning 'to love', and *dendron*, meaning 'tree', because many philodendrons are superb tree-climbers and they are often sold as houseplants with a coir trunk for the developing plant to climb up. In the wild, they can grow to extraordinary heights, and – looked after well and in ideal conditions – they can become quite unruly as houseplants, too. That's the perfect time to propagate them and regift for friends and family.

The method we describe here can be used for most trailing plants, so, next time you have to trim a wayward specimen, try propagating it instead!

You Will Need

— Pots (one for each node
   you want to propagate)
— Potting mix
— Paperclips
— Sharp knife

How to Propagate

Heart-leaf Philodendron

1 — Identify which stem of the plant you want to propagate from. Fill the pots with potting mix.

2 — If necessary, move the plant from its regular place, since you'll need space to lay out the propagation stem. Place the pots out in a row beside the parent plant.

3 — Place your chosen stem along the top of the pots, spacing them underneath it so that the nodes (the places where the leaves join the stem) fall where the pots are.

4 — For each pot, empty out a little of the potting mix, bury the stem – holding it down with an opened-out paperclip if necessary – and refill the hole. It doesn't need to be buried too deep, and in fact the tension in the stem will limit how deep you can bury it. If your plant is leggy, with few nodes, make a shallow scratch on the underside of the stem with a knife before burying it, but do this only on the section of stem that will be in contact with the potting mix. The idea is to encourage the formation of a root nodule.

5 Water each pot and make sure it drains properly. Now all you have to do is wait.

6 Within six to eight weeks you should start to see the new plant pushing up from the underside of the stem. Once its leaves begin to unfurl, the root system will have formed and you can cut it free. To play it safe, wait until each new propagation (those that have taken) is at the stage where the leaves have opened up before cutting it free.

Plant Care

Water	The heart-leaf philodendron originally comes from the Caribbean, Colombia and Venezuela, and is therefore used to heat, humidity and intermittent watering. In the lower temperatures of most homes it can tolerate drying out, and in fact it does not like to sit in water at all.
Food	A houseplant feed once a fortnight in spring and summer is plenty.
Light	Philodendron likes a light, bright spot, but won't be happy in full sun.
Care	It is quite rare for philodendron to flower when houseplants, but if this does happen, cut off the blooms – they drain a lot of energy from the plant and don't smell very good at all.
Note	Philodendron can be toxic if eaten, so it is not safe to grow if you have small children or pets.

Snake Plant

(Dracaena trifasciata)
Whole-leaf cutting (without petiole)

The snake plant is one of the most popular houseplants in the world, and it's not difficult to see why. It's an absolute beauty, with sharp, graphic lines and exotically patterned leaves. It's the sharp lines that have left the snake plant with some unkind old nicknames, not least of them 'mother-in-law's tongue', from the lazy old trope of this beloved family member's reputation for barbed comments ...

The key to the snake plant's success is the easy nature with which it grows. You can ignore your plant for weeks and it will be just fine. In fact, it's best practice to let the snake plant dry out between waterings. So, if you're away a lot, or just plain forgetful, this is the houseplant for you.

Here we describe how to propagate the snake plant in water and in soil. The latter method is a lot slower, but requires less effort on your part. We like to propagate whole leaves this way, because they look like a normal and healthy snake plant even while they are rooting, and can be treated in more or less the same way. It makes the propagation less onerous and creates a lovely feature along the way.

You Will Need

— Sharp knife
— Hormone rooting powder
— Potting mix
— Plant pot

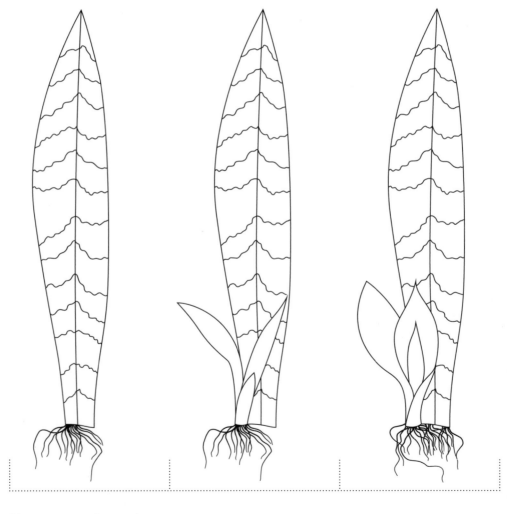

How to Propagate

Snake Plant

1   Look for a leaf to propagate. The most successful specimens are those that look healthy (shiny skin, rigid habit, brightly coloured) and are fully grown, but not too old. Cut the leaf free at the base.

2   You can leave the leaf whole or, if it is large enough, cut it into sections (potentially giving you more plants). Each section should be about 8cm (3¼in) long. (In our experience, the snake-plant pups form more quickly when they are grown from a complete leaf.) To keep track of which end of the leaf is 'up', you can mark an arrow on each cutting with permanent marker.

3   Once you've cut the leaf or the sections, leave them to air-dry for a day or two, until a skin forms on the cut edges.

4   Before you pot on the dried-out cuttings, dip the lower end (the root side of the cutting) in water, just to wet the edge, and then in hormone rooting powder, to encourage propagation.

5   Fill the pot with potting mix, water thoroughly and let it drain.

6

Push the cuttings into the potting mix until they are about 2cm (¾in) deep, or deeper if you are using a whole-leaf cutting.

7

To help prevent rot, let the potting mix dry out before watering again. The rooting process will take a Herculean effort of patience, since it can be a full year before the pups can be potted on as separate plants.

Tip

Snake plants can also be propagated in water: place the dried-out sections upright in a jar with enough water to cover the cut end by 1–2cm (about ¾in). They must be placed the same way up as they were on the parent plant; that is to say, the lower end of the leaf should go in the water.

Now you just have to wait until you see roots and then a small snake plant begin to form along the cut edge of the leaf. The most important thing during this time is to keep the water fresh. It will need changing at least once a week. When you do so, take the cutting out and feel it below the waterline. If it feels at all slimy, rinse it under the tap (faucet), wash the glass and change the water. You might even want to rub the slime away lightly with your fingers as you wash it.

Rotting can be a real problem with snake plants because it can take two months, or even longer, for roots to form. Be prepared for the long haul!

Plant Care

Water	Let the potting mix dry out between waterings. In winter, a once-a-month water will be plenty.
Food	This is a very slow-growing plant and therefore requires a feed only once at the beginning of spring and again at the beginning of summer. Use liquid feed at half strength.
Light	Snake plants can tolerate a wide range of light conditions.
Care	One of the reasons the snake plant is so resilient is that the pores on its leaves open only at night, allowing it to retain water. Therefore, wiping its leaves down with a damp cloth will keep it happy and help it to breathe.
Note	If your parent plant is variegated, the baby plants will lose the variegated edge. If you want to retain the look for the next generation you'll need to divide the plant as you would the aspidistra (see page 21).

Propagate

Rubber Plant
(Ficus elastica)
Tip cuttings

The rubber plant goes by a few different names, including rubber fig, rubber tree and Indian rubber bush. When we were kids in the 1980s, rubber plants tended to be leggy, dusty hangovers from another era. They'd lurk worryingly in the corners of dentists' waiting rooms and stuffy travel agents' offices. It was almost enough to put you off rubber for life.

Since then, and thanks to seductive TV period dramas such as *Mad Men*, the rubber plant has made a comeback along with mid-century furniture and dirty martinis. Now it's one of those plants that can turn an empty room into a designer space. Its lush, round leaves are already giving the popular fiddle-leaf fig (see page 131) a run for its money.

Happily, rubber plants are really easy to propagate, so if you're in the mood for free love (and free plants) this is a great place to start. An indoor rubber plant will need pruning once in a while, so this is the perfect time to turn those pruned cuttings into brand-new plants.

You Will Need

- — Secateurs or pruning knife
- — 10cm (4in)-diameter plant pot
- — Potting mix
- — Hormone rooting powder (optional)
- — Pencil (optional)
- — Clear plastic crate with lid
- — Drill and suitable bit
- — Water mister

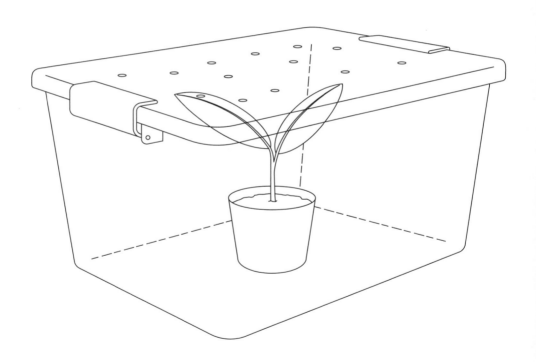

How to Propagate

Rubber Plant

1	Using the secateurs or a pruning knife, cut a section of branch from the mother plant, measuring about 15cm (6in) long and containing two sets of leaves.
2	Carefully remove the bottom set of leaves, leaving the top leaves intact.
3	Leave the cutting to dry somewhere out of direct sunlight for 24 hours. This step should help to avoid bacterial infections in the wound of the cutting.
4	Fill the new plant pot with potting mix and dampen the soil with fresh, clean water.
5	Dip the cutting into hormone rooting powder, if you like, and tap off any excess. Now use your finger, or a pencil, to make a hole about 5cm (2in) deep in the potting mix, and insert the cutting.

6 Place the pot in a clear plastic crate with several air holes drilled in the lid. This will act as a mini greenhouse over the coming days and weeks to replicate a tropical climate.

7 Place the crate in a temperate space in your house, with indirect sunlight.

8 Over the next two or three weeks, keep the potting mix slightly damp but well drained by watering sparingly if needed and misting the interior of the crate with fresh water every few days.

9 By week three, your plant should have started to establish its own root system and will be ready to begin its journey as a strong, independent houseplant. If, after several weeks, you are still unsure as to whether your cutting has 'taken' we suggest gently tugging the stem. If there's resistance then the roots are growing as they should.

Plant Care

Water	Rubber plants prefer well-drained soil, but over the growing season it's best to pay a little extra attention to keeping the soil properly moist. If you're planning to keep your plant in a particularly dry environment (central heating or air-conditioning can cause this), it's a good idea to spritz the air around the plant with fresh water once in a while to increase the humidity.
Food	Rubber plants like a high-phosphorus fertiliser monthly during the spring and summer months when they do the majority of their growing.
Light	Bright but indirect light.
Temperature	Standard room temperature is perfect.
Care	Over time this plant will try to grow tall and leggy, but it responds well to being pruned into shape. To help it take shape further, you can encourage new leaf growth by nicking or lightly slicing a leaf scar (a leaf scar is a line where a leaf previously grew). When it's time to repot the rubber plant, don't be tempted to increase the pot size too much in one go. Rubber plants like their soil compact, so choose a new pot that's only about 2.5cm (1in) larger than the last. Now sit back and enjoy a martini.

Propagate

Golden Pothos

(Epipremnum aureum)

Ground-layering

Pothos, often known as devil's ivy because of its ability to do well in the darkest places, is an easy-going and reliable houseplant. Its cascading leaves and branches can add drama to a bookcase or shelf, and during the summer the sheer speed of growth is satisfying to watch.

There's a broad mix of varieties, each with their own shape and colour. Some of the best-known are marble queen, neon pothos and jessenia. If you are in the process of growing a living wall, incorporating a variety of pothos can add the colour, movement and texture you're looking for. But leaves are definitely the main attraction: pothos very rarely flowers without being pumped with hormones. Aptly, the last reported spontaneous flowering was during the Flower Power movement of the 1960s.

The most straightforward method of propagating this plant is a simple stem cutting (as for monstera; see page 33), but we thought we'd show you another method that you might prefer to try: ground-layering. This is a method that can be used on any plant with flexible stems, as it involves bending the living stems down to a potting mix to encourage new sections of root. The benefit of ground-layering is that the newly rooting baby plant continues to receive nutrients and water from the mother plant as it grows.

You Will Need

— Small plant pot
— Potting mix
— Paperclip
— Gardening scissors or pruning knife

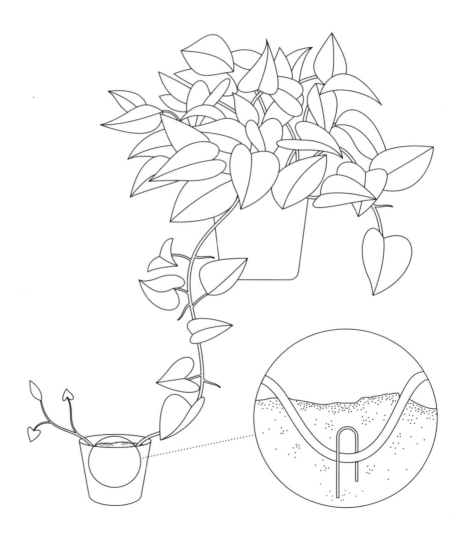

How to Propagate

Golden Pothos

1   Fill the pot with potting mix. This will be the home for your newly propagated plant.

2   Select a healthy vine or branch from the mother plant – one that's long enough to reach the new pot.

3   Leaving the stem attached to the main plant, identify a section containing a node (a node is a small light-coloured bump coming off the plant's green stem) and secure this to the soil of the smaller pot using an opened-out paperclip.

4   Water the smaller pot as you would the mother plant, but with extra care not to let the potting mix dry out.

5   Once the ground-layering has worked, you'll begin to see new leaf growth from the pinned section of vine. Closer inspection should reveal that new roots have formed on the baby plant. At that point you can separate the new plant from the mother plant by cutting it free using gardening scissors or a pruning knife.

Propagate

Plant Care

Water	Pothos requires a moderate amount of water, so let the top 5cm (2in) of soil dry out between waterings. Too much water will result in dark brown spots on the leaves.
Food	A liquid fertiliser every few months works best.
Light	Pothos can tolerate low light, although varieties with streaked or variegated leaves will need a brighter position to retain their colours.
Temperature	Pothos originates in warm environments, so it prefers temperatures of 18–30°C (65–85°F) and around 85 per cent humidity.
Care	Remember to prune your pothos plant to encourage growth and vitality. Don't be afraid to get stuck in – they thrive on drama.
Also try this with	Goosefoot plant (*Syngonium podophyllum*) and anthurium

Propagate

Lavender

(Lavandula)

Heel cutting

We have bundles of lavender at the allotment. We love the colour and scent in high summer, but it's the bees that really go crazy for those rich purple and lilac blooms – and they're every gardener's best friends. We could sit with an ice-cold glass of one of our fruit wines and watch the bees busily harvesting the pollen for days. Nothing feels more like summer.

At the beginning of summer 2021, we moved to a new allotment plot that backed on to the river but it was in a terrible state. Paul had the idea of planting a row of lavender all the way down the middle of the plot, edging an existing brick path. To surprise him, Robin bought a few lavender plants to cannibalise into cuttings so that we could plant up his dramatic idea and save ourselves a fortune in the process. The ideal time to do it is late summer, so that the cuttings are mature enough.

Once your propagations have established themselves, why not bring them inside for the summer? They'll thrive on a bright sill in direct light.

You Will Need

— Small pots (we used 10cm/4in diameter pots)
— Potting mix
— Sharp knife
— Hormone rooting powder
— Clear plastic bags
— Elastic bands or string

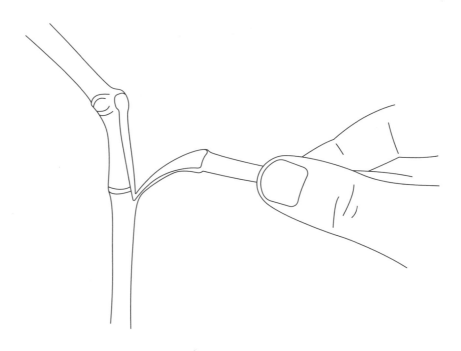

How to Propagate
Lavender

1 First, prepare your pots by filling them with potting mix.

2 You'll need to take your cuttings from the stems that make up this year's growth. You can recognise them because they'll still be green, not woody – gardeners call them 'semi-ripe cuttings'. Ideally, choose stems that have not flowered and that are at least a month old. If they are flowering, cut off the flowers cleanly at the base of the flower stalk.

3 This is called a heel cutting because it should have a 'heel' at the bottom. This simply looks a little like the heel of your foot, and it is made by pulling the cutting away from the main stem, rather than chopping it off. Pull gently, down towards the ground and away from the main stem. Once your cutting comes away you'll see a little thread of rind that pulls away from the donor stem, and that's the heel. If some of your cuttings don't have a heel – which will happen sometimes – use them anyway, rather than wasting them as they may still take root.

4 Remove the lower leaves by pulling them away and down towards the cut end of the cutting, or slicing them off with a sharp knife. Remove enough that, when the time comes, the cutting can be pushed into the potting mix deep enough to stand upright, without any leaves touching the potting mix.

5

Dip the heel in water and then hormone rooting powder, and tap away any excess.

6

Push the cuttings into the potting mix, two or three to each pot. Then firm down the potting mix, water generously and allow to drain.

7

Once the excess water has drained away, put a small plastic bag over the top of the pot and secure it with an elastic band or string. The bag must be big enough for the lavender to stand upright inside it without touching the plastic.

8

Put this 'mini-propagator' somewhere warm and in partial shade to work its magic, and keep checking the cuttings for drying out, overheating or bugs. After four to six weeks they should start to root, at which stage you can remove the bag and harden the plants off.

9

Once your new plants are well rooted, pot them up individually and overwinter them inside. Come spring they'll burst back into life, ready for planting in the ground.

Plant Care

Water	Lavender is native to the Mediterranean and so is well suited to grow as a houseplant under certain conditions. Water is one of the things to be most mindful of: the pot should have pebbles or pottery shards at the bottom to help with drainage. Let the soil dry out between watering so that the top 2cm (¾in) are bone dry. The lavender will need only the occasional water over winter and perhaps as much as once a week in high summer.
Food	It will only need a liquid houseplant feed twice a year – once at the start of the growing season and again in mid-summer.
Light	Is hugely important. They must be in direct sunlight for a good few hours a day, no less than 3–4 hours.
Care	Lavender likes it hot but be careful it isn't baked to death on a windowsill suntrap. Glazing and ceramic pots can get very hot so be aware of the extremes your plant may be put through while you're at work!
Also try this with	Rosemary

Peace Lily

(Spathiphyllum wallisii)

Seed

In the 1980s, NASA conducted a study into which houseplants are best at purifying the air. The goal was to find the most effective ways to clean the atmosphere in space stations. The peace lily outperformed almost all its rivals, successfully removing even chemicals such as benzene and trichloroethylene from the air. Another reason NASA got all starry-eyed about this houseplant is its tolerance of very low light – perfect if you live in an orbiting space pod, or an inner-city basement apartment for that matter.

The peace lily gives us a chance to try our hand at good old-fashioned sexual propagation, just as nature intended. It's true that the easiest way of propagating this plant is by dividing the roots (which is known as vegetative or asexual propagation), but the more exciting challenge is to pollinate a peace lily manually with the aim of collecting its seeds.

Growing your own peace lily (which in truth isn't really a lily) from seed might be rewarding, but, unlike with asexual propagation – which effectively produces clones – sexual propagation means your new baby peace lily might vary from its mother plant. Don't let this thought put you off; it's all part of the fun. Of course, you'll need to wait for your plant to produce flowers before you can begin the process. Once you notice them, it's time to spring into action.

Note that if your plant is producing one flower at a time, you'll need to follow some steps to retain pollen from one flower to fertilise the female parts of the next emerging flower. The flower's female parts are receptive to pollen before the flower produces pollen itself, so you have to perform a little trickery to make this work.

You Will Need

— Paper envelopes
— Small, soft paintbrush
— Gardening scissors
— Tweezers
— Seed tray
— Vermiculite
— Watering can
— Cling film (plastic wrap)
— Pots and potting mix, for potting on

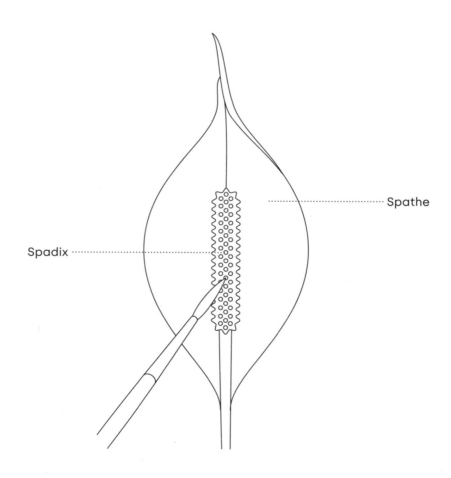

Spadix

Spathe

How to Propagate

Peace Lily

To obtain seed

1   First, we need to collect the plant's pollen. The peace lily 'flower' is technically something called an inflorescence, which is made up of a spadix (the sharp cone in the middle) and the spathe (the outside cover, which resembles a petal). Keep an eye on the spadix, as, about 24 hours after the spathe unfurls, this part of the plant will start to turn brown and produce the pollen.

2   The actual flowers of the peace lily are tiny and run all the way down the spadix, and it's these little blooms that produce the pollen. When you are confident that pollen is being produced, bring a clean envelope close to the spadix and gently tap the flower stalk to capture the yellow powder.

3   Seal the envelope and store it safely in a cool, dry place. It should stay fresh for at least a few weeks, until you are ready for the next step.

4   If your plant has several 'flowers' opening at once, press ahead with the next step immediately; otherwise, wait for a second 'flower' to emerge from the plant. As the spathe unfurls, oh so seductively, the plant's female parts become ready to be pollinated (and just for a 24-hour window, too). If the tiny flowers on the spadix have a fine fuzz on them and are yet to turn brown, the time is right.

5   Love is in the air. Use the paintbrush to apply the pollen from the envelope gently all over the spadix.

6 It may take many days or weeks, but you should notice the flowers on the spadix beginning to swell as the peace lily starts to produce fruit. A spadix bearing fruit will turn brown and continue to dry out, eventually becoming a blackened seed pod. Use gardening scissors to remove the pod from the plant by snipping the stem away at its base.

7 Using a clean pair of tweezers, carefully remove the round seeds from the pod, collecting them in an envelope for safe keeping. Store the envelope in a cool, dark, dry place until you are ready to plant the seeds.

To grow a peace lily from seed

1 Fill a seed tray with vermiculite and use a watering can to gently shower the tray until it's well moistened. Then distribute the seeds evenly on top.

2 Sprinkle a little more vermiculite on top of the seeds, to make a light top layer, and water again very carefully, trying not to displace the seeds.

3 Cover the tray with a piece of cling film to create a greenhouse effect around the seeds, then place the entire tray in bright but indirect light.

4 Over the coming days it's advisable to keep the seeds moist by bottom-watering the tray: allow the tray to stand in water for 30 minutes whenever it appears to be drying out. If you're lucky, your seeds will start to germinate after about two weeks, but they might take much longer than this, so don't be too hasty to think you've failed.

5 Once the seedlings are large enough to handle, transfer them to pots of their own. Growing on is relatively simple, provided you take care not to let these tropical plants dry out in their youth.

Plant Care

Water	A good indication that you aren't watering a peace lily enough is drooping leaves. You can use this as an initial guide to understand how often your plant needs to be watered. Make sure it never sits in standing water.
Food	These plants only need an occasional dose of houseplant fertiliser.
Light	Low to bright light suits the peace lily, but be sure not to let its leaves scorch by siting it in full sun.
Temperature	Peace lilies come from a tropical environment, so don't let them get too cold. They also love humidity, so if you are seeking a plant for the bathroom, this is a good choice.

ZZ Plant

(Zamioculcas zamiifolia)

Leaf cutting

ZZ (pronounced 'Zee-Zee', American-style) originally comes from East Africa, and was first described in the West by local horticultural legend Conrad Loddiges (see page 150). He noted, way back in 1828, that '[*Zamioculcas zamiifolia* is a] very singular and curious plant which we believe to be a native of Brazil'. (Well, I guess you can't get everything right.) He went on to describe the strange ground-lying flower and the fact that it bloomed in August, after he had 'preserved the plant in the stove', which was probably the name for the warmest part of his nursery complex, rather than an actual oven.

We've classed this as a medium propagation, although it is fairly simple to do because the ZZ plant is desperate to be propagated. The only thing that's at all tricky is the time your propagated cuttings will take to grow more shoots and establish. If you follow our method, you really won't have to do much at all, but it'll be up to a year before you can pot your ZZ plants on individually, and during that time you'll need to keep an eye on the propagator. So it's not as simple as it might at first sound.

In yet another flaw of nomenclature we've called this a leaf cutting, but it's really a 'partial' leaf cutting, since each frond that you see above ground is one leaf, with a central petiole (stalk). What you may have thought of as leaves are actually 'leaflets', and it's these that you'll be propagating.

You Will Need

— Sharp knife
— Pot or tray (almost every leaflet can be propagated, so choose a container large enough to take them all)
— Potting mix
— Ziplock bag
— Water mister

How to Propagate

ZZ Plant

1   Cut a frond from the parent plant at the base.

2   Now it's time to choose your leaflets. Don't use any that are damaged or diseased, have pests or look in any way less healthy than the others. There should be plenty to choose from, so be picky. Pull up and down on your chosen leaflet. You'll get the feel of it, and, after a bit of pressure in both directions, the leaflet will snap off in your hand.

3   Work your way along the stem, removing as many leaflets as you intend to propagate. When you've finished, discard what's left.

4   Fill the pot or tray with potting mix to a depth of at least 5cm (2in). Water thoroughly and leave to drain.

5   Push each leaflet upright into the potting mix to a depth of 1–2cm (½–¾in), stalk first, and firm the potting mix around it. It should be deep enough to hold its position.

6   Water the leaflets and again leave to drain.

7   Put the pot or tray in a ziplock bag and seal it. Place the bag in a warm, bright spot, out of direct sunlight, and check at least twice a week that the potting mix remains moist. If it appears to be drying out, mist the surface with water.

8 The leaflets should all stay green, so, when you check their progress, remove any that have yellowed or browned. Otherwise, all you need do now is wait.

9 The plant will form a type of solid root below the surface before it sends up any leaves, so after a few months you can do a tug test to see if it has rooted. To do this, simply pull the leaflet gently. If you feel some resistance to it coming out of the soil, it has rooted. Now all you need is patience.

10 About a year after you began your propagation, the first of the new leaflets should begin to emerge. There will be only a couple of leaflets on this first leaf. Once the plants are large enough to handle, pot them on individually.

11 After 18 months, each propagated plant should have a healthy set of perhaps as many as 10 leaflets.

Plant Care

Water	In the wild ZZs, are fed by heavy, infrequent rains, so ideally let the potting mix dry out completely between waterings. In winter this may mean leaving a couple of months between drinks.
Food	This plant only needs the occasional feed, perhaps once every four to six weeks and only during spring and summer.
Light	Even though the ZZ plant comes from Africa, it can cope with very low light levels, so it's ideal for a dim corner away from any windows.
Note	Happy and healthy, your ZZ plant will grow quite large. A mature specimen might reach a height of nearly 1m (3ft).

The Perpetual Propagator

On a sunny day in July, we met up with Fraser Cook, a horticulturist and RHS (Royal Horticultural Society) Diploma student, to hear his views on propagation and cultivation.

Your Instagram account, @botanicalotter, is packed with plants. When did you first fall in love with them?

Through my twenties and thirties I was completely focused on my career, but the love of plants has gradually crept in. Like many others, the time spent at home during the COVID-19 pandemic enhanced my gardening aspirations.

In truth, I actually find the large number of plants in my life quite stressful! As beautiful as they are, more houseplants mean more responsibility. It's a joyful process, but it's not without its pressure.

Then what's the big attraction?

The sense of community is huge for me – and I love the intergenerational aspect. Online, gardening enthusiasts and plant-lovers are always talking to one another, sharing ideas and passing on tips. There's no one right answer to any given question, and opinion differs wildly, so there's always something to talk about. But you can't argue with botany, and I learn a lot from true botanists, soil scientists and horticulturists all over the world.

What do you think about the 'plant revolution' that's taken place over recent years?

If you mean the sudden increase in interest in plants, then of course I think it's great that more people, especially younger people, have got involved. I mean, plants are all over social media and you can see people forming their own sense of celebrity around their plant collection and creating content around that.

As much as it's a great thing to get plant-obsessed, it's worthwhile using that energy to learn more about where your plants have come from, take some gardening courses and consider sustainability. I guess it's time we used social media to educate about horticulture, and drive awareness about conservation, joining up the houseplant community with that of the gardening world.

Tell us about your popping seeds?

I noticed that my spring anemone seed pods were about to release, so I collected what I could, but instead of storing them in an airtight container, I put them in a paper envelope and they exploded brilliantly inside.

You learn that plants have their own unique methods of dispersal, from catapulting to exploding. In the past I've had to soak seeds in juice to mimic the gut acid of animals, or keep them in warm baths of water for 24 hours. A lot goes into seed propagation and, surprisingly, some common garden flowers are actually really hard to germinate. But it's worth it.

Hard

Propagate

Wax Begonia

(Begonia x semperflorens-cultorum)

Whole-leaf split-vein propagation

Since 1988, a begonia cultivar named 'Kimjongilia' has been the unofficial floral emblem of North Korea! Its name means 'the flower of Kim Jong-il', after the country's then 'Supreme Leader', the father of the current despot. The flower was chosen to represent wisdom, love, justice and peace ...

The begonias are a huge family of diverse plants that come from many tropical regions of the world, so if 'Kimjongilia' isn't your thing, you're sure to find one that is. We love them as bedding as well as houseplants, which can last for years under ideal conditions and care.

Begonias have some of the smallest seeds in the plant kingdom; just 30g (1oz) of seed is enough to grow up to three million begonias! However, propagating from seed is nowhere near as much fun as growing new plants using the whole-leaf split-vein propagation technique, and the wax begonia variety is particularly well suited to this kind of propagation. The large veins and waxy sheen mean the cuts are easier to make, protecting the leaf from rot (which some begonia varieties can be susceptible to).

You Will Need

— Vermiculite
— Enough pots of the right size for your leaf cuttings
— Sharp knife
— Hormone rooting powder and paper towel (optional, but recommended)
— Fine gravel, sand, paperclips (optional) or cocktail sticks (toothpicks), sterilised with boiling water
— Clear plastic bag for each pot
— Elastic bands or string

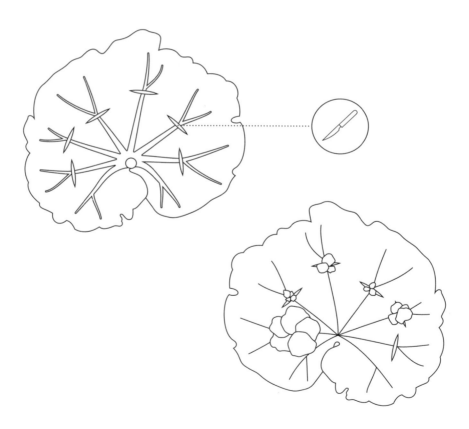

How to Propagate

Wax Begonia

1

First, clean all the plastic equipment you will be using with warm soapy water, or, if it is heat-safe, pour boiling water over it and leave to cool.

2

Half-fill the pots – making sure they have a large enough surface area for your leaf or leaves to lie flat – with vermiculite (you need to leave enough headroom for the plantlets to grow, but it can be shallow; a depth of 5cm/2in is plenty). Water well and leave to drain. We recommend using one pot for each cutting. That will limit the chances of rot spoiling a whole batch.

3

Select a mature, healthy leaf that is fully formed but not getting old. Just like us humans, plants lose a bit of their razzle-dazzle as they age (which may be why you are propagating the plant in the first place), and the older the leaves are, the more difficult they are to propagate – basically, they're done with reproduction.

4

Using the knife, remove a leaf from the main plant, making the cut where the leaf meets the stem, so the leaf can lie flat with its underside facing upwards. You'll see that veins track across the underside of the leaf, starting at the main central vein and dividing repeatedly across the leaf, getting smaller each time, until they become too fine to see.

5

Where the veins branch off the main vein, you will see that each divides into two, before continuing across the leaf and dividing again. This is where you should make the cuts, just before (meaning towards the main vein and the middle of the leaf) the place where each vein divides into two for the first time. Make a small incision with the knife, simply severing each of these first branched veins.

6 Sprinkle some of the rooting powder, if using, on to a paper towel and press the leaf into it so that the powder sticks to the cut edges. Tap off any excess.

7 Turn the leaf the right way up and place it on the surface of the vermiculite. It may curl away from the surface, in which case use the vermiculite or some fine gravel or sand to hold it down. This is essential, since the cut veins must be in contact with the vermiculite. You can also use a bent-open paper clip or cocktail sticks to pin the leaf down. Try not to damage the leaf too much.

8 Alternatively, you can cut the leaf into postage stamp-sized pieces, making sure each one contains a section of the main vein. Dust the edges with hormone powder and pot up as in step 7.

9 Cover the pot with a sterile plastic bag secured with an elastic band or string.

10 Now, you need to keep the vermiculite moist and wait. It can take three months for the new plants to start to grow at the cut veins, so this stage requires patience, but after a few weeks you should see roots starting to form. Once the plantlets are about 1cm (½in) tall you can remove the plastic to acclimatise them before potting them on.

11 When they are large enough to handle, the plantlets can be potted on individually and hardened off ready for life outside the propagator.

Plant Care

Water	Wax begonias must be kept moist. Ideally, water into the drip tray most of the time, and only occasionally at the pot's surface, to reduce the chances of fungal disease. You will find that you can reduce the amount of watering drastically in winter.
Food	Every two weeks or so in spring and summer.
Light	Bright but indirect sunlight is perfect for begonias.
Care	Begonias are very easy to look after. Deadhead them to keep them producing more blooms, and pinch out the tips to keep the plant nice and compact – if that's what you want.
Also try this with	Gloxinia *(Sinningia)* and temple bells *(Smithiantha)*

Propagate

Fiddle-leaf Fig

(Ficus lyrata)

Air-layering

Don't you think the fiddle-leaf fig looks too good to be true? It's like one of those plastic trees at a shopping mall. Its large, glossy leaves give this fig a majesty that few other houseplants can muster, and that's why we love it.

A large fiddle-leaf fig can be a very expensive houseplant to buy new, which makes it a lovely gift. Although a propagated plant will be slow-growing at first, within a few years you'll have saved yourself – or the propagated plant's recipient – a small fortune. Robin's was given to him as a cutting by his friends James and Olly, whose beautiful parent specimen thrives in their apartment. Its architectural shape perfectly complements the industrial vibe they've designed for themselves.

Air-layering is ideal for propagating the fiddle-leaf fig, which has long, thick, woody stems. Even though it can be simply propagated by a tip or leaf cutting in a glass of water, you get a medium-sized plant more quickly from an air-layered propagation – if a year can ever be described as quick!

You Will Need

— Sharp knife
— Gardening gloves (optional)
— Cocktail stick (toothpick)
— Hormone rooting powder (optional)
— Coco coir soaked in water for an hour and wrung
   out tightly using clean hands
— Spare pair of hands!
— Sheet of clear, flexible polythene 30cm (12in)
   square
— String
— Secateurs
— Plant pot (at least 20cm/8in diameter)
— Potting mix

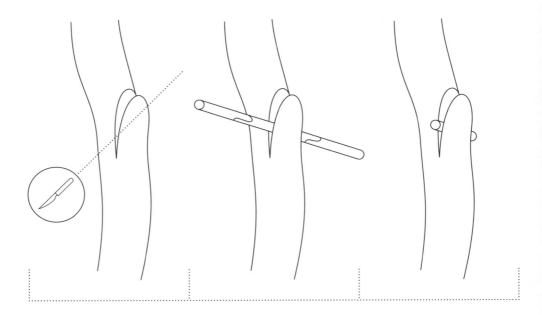

How to Propagate

Fiddle-leaf Fig

1 Identify a long section of stem to make the air-layer. First, wound the bark on the stem by cutting into the branch with your knife. Cut no deeper than between one third and half the way into the stem. The stem will be woody and hard to cut, so be very careful. It's easy for the knife to slip and cut you at this point, as we can testify. Always use the knife in a motion that is away from you and, especially, away from your fingers.

2 To help the wound stay open, press the cocktail stick (dipped in hormone rooting powder first) into the cut, sideways. This will force the cut open and get the powder right to where it's needed.

3 Trim the cocktail stick so that it no longer pokes out from the sides of the stem, otherwise it may tear the polythene and act as a source of secondary infection.

4 Take a handful of the coco coir a little smaller than a tennis ball, and press it around the wounded stem.

5 Hold the coir ball in place while your accomplice wraps the polythene around the coir, holding both plastic and coir around the wounded stem. You can see how this needs more than one pair of hands!

6 While holding the plastic in place, check the wound is still in the middle of the coir and tie string tightly around the lower end of the ball of coir – now partially wrapped in plastic.

7

Make sure the coir is still tightly packed, the plastic is wrapped tightly and the string is holding the ball in place at the bottom before making a tie at the top in the same way. The ties must be tight enough to retain moisture, so that the coir doesn't dry out too quickly. (If this happens – which it will eventually – pour a little water in through the top of the plastic, to dampen the coir again.)

8

And that's it – all that's left to do is wait. Condensation will form on the inside of the plastic, but this is perfectly normal. Keep checking the air-layer and eventually you should be able to make out roots growing through the coir. It can take a few months, so be patient!

9

Once the stem has rooted, remove the string and polythene to reveal a healthy network of roots. Using secateurs, cut the plantlet free of the mother plant below the place where the roots have formed.

10

Pot it up immediately in potting mix and water generously. Make sure it's in a big enough pot and buried to an appropriate depth to stay upright.

Tip

When you cut into the fiddle-leaf fig you'll notice a sticky cream-coloured liquid oozing from the stem. This is a perfectly natural type of rubber (the fiddle-leaf fig is part of the rubber-plant family), but it can be an irritant, so wear gloves if you have sensitive skin. Make sure it doesn't get smeared everywhere, since it can be difficult to remove.

Plant Care

Water	This type of fig loves humidity, so it must be kept away from radiators and spritzed regularly (this is also the perfect opportunity to keep those luscious waxy leaves free of dust). However, it also prefers to dry out a little between waterings, so check that the top 5cm (2in) of soil is dry to the touch before watering generously. This should be about once a week in summer; it'll need a lot less water in winter.
Food	Feed your fiddle-leaf fig once every couple of weeks in spring and summer.
Light	Bright, indirect light is best.
Note	Some people recommend wiggling your fig tree from side to side for a minute each day. Not too vigorously – you're trying to emulate a gentle breeze. This will help to build a strong root and a thicker stem, since they can grow quite leggy. If once a day is too much for you, just do it when you remember or can be bothered.

Propagate

Hart's-tongue Fern
(Asplenium scolopendrium)
Propagating from spores

Ferns are sexier than you ever imagined. These plants are ancient, dating back hundreds of millions of years, which means that, unlike most of the plant life that surrounds us today, they were trampled on and nibbled at by dinosaurs! They are so ancient that they don't reproduce in the same way as the more evolutionarily advanced (and modern) flowering plants, and that is what makes them so fun to propagate.

Ferns exist as two generations that form separately and look completely different, making propagating them a bit of a challenge. Think of this 'alternation of generations' between one kind of plant and another as like if humans gave birth to squirrel children, who in turn grew up and had human babies ... How crazy is that? With ferns we only ever see the sporophyte or 'true fern' generation – unless you are propagating them, in which case you get a front-row seat for one of nature's miracles.

Robin chose to propagate the hart's-tongue fern because the plants remind him of his native Devon and the shaded banks of country lanes there, which are lined with ferns, this type in particular.

The term 'sporophyte' means 'spore-holding', and in high summer you'll see little ridge-like structures on the underside of the hart's-tongue's leaves (although in ferns, the leaves are actually called fronds). These ridges are the maturing spores, and collecting them is the first stage in this propagation.

Green spores are still immature and need time to develop. But once they've changed to brown (black on some fern species), you are good to go. The tip of each frond will have the least mature spores, and the base of the frond the ripest. There's a knack to telling if the spores are just right. Once they've changed colour, the spore 'pockets' should look fresh with neat edges, and not old, mottled or shrivelled.

You Will Need

— Sharp knife
— White envelope
— Jam (jelly) jars and lids or Kilner (Mason) jars/ clip jars
— Potting mix (coir-free, since ferns don't like coir)
— Vermiculite
— Water mister
— Boiled and cooled water
— Teaspoon or large tweezers
— Tray or pots for potting on
— Ziplock bags (large enough to contain the pot and then some)

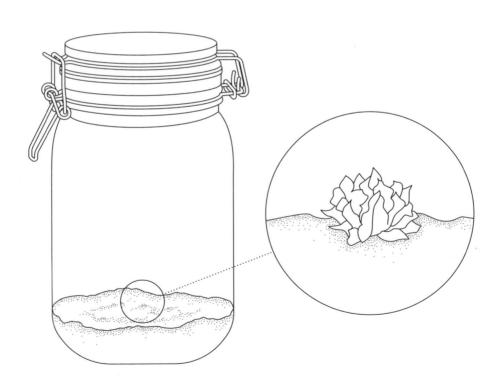

How to Propagate

Hart's-tongue Fern

1   Cut off your chosen fern frond and store it in a white envelope somewhere dry and warm for a few days (we use our kitchen drawers). When you're ready, shake or flick the envelope to dislodge the spores. If you're propagating more than one species of fern, use a different envelope for each one so you don't mix up the spores.

2   Open the envelope and you'll see the spores as a fine, almost powder-like dust against the paper (that's why we recommend using a white envelope). Remove the frond and tap the envelope to separate the (larger) casing from the (finer) spores. With a bit of practice you should notice the casing falling from the envelope while the tiny, dust-like spores stay on the surface of the paper.

3   Fill the jars to a depth of 3–5cm (1–2in) with the potting mix, then sprinkle the vermiculite on top, covering about half the surface area of the potting mix, in a thin layer to a depth of 0.5cm (¼in).

4   Spritz the surface of the vermiculite with boiled and cooled water until it's damp but not wet.

5   Open the envelope out flat and tap it until the dry spores drop into the jars. There should be thousands of them, so try to distribute them by eye as best you can. (This is why flowering plants evolved – reproducing from spores is very wasteful and requires many millions of spores to make a limited number of new plants.)

Propagate

6 Seal the jars tightly and put them on a windowsill or other warm, bright place, but not in direct sunlight. After a while you'll see condensation form on the inside, and this is essential.

7 We advise keeping a close eye on the jars at first, to make sure the potting mix doesn't dry out. If it does, quickly add another good spritz of boiled, cooled water. Apart from that, you just need to leave everything well alone and let nature take its course.

8 The first thing that will happen is that tiny green dots will appear, after roughly 4–6 weeks. These dots will multiply and expand to form a green mossy fuzz that will cover the surface. This is good – it's the 'squirrel' generation forming! This will take a month or more to fill in.

9 These tiny plants now need to reproduce with themselves to make the following generation, the recognisable – although at this stage tiny – ferns. This next stage takes anything between two and six months, but luckily you don't have to do anything much: simply make sure the little 'squirrels' and then their 'human' babies don't dry out.

10 Once the mossy 'leaves' are roughly 0.5cm (¼in) across, it is time to 'patch out' – to transfer clumps of the mossy mat to a tray or larger pots to grow on. Using a teaspoon or large tweezers, simply cut the mat into clumps where you can see the new larger plants protruding from it, and space them evenly 3–4cm (1¼–1½in) apart in a grid on potting mix.

11 Spray the transplants vigorously with boiled and cooled water, then bag them up in clean, clear ziplock bags. (You can skip this stage and let the process continue in the jar, but it may mean that fewer ferns mature.)

12 Put the pots or tray back into the bright spot and leave for between one and four months. The time this next stage takes will depend on the species.

13   In time you will see a new type of plant structure begin to emerge from the 'squirrel' generation. This is the sporophyte generation again (like the original plant) – the true fern. You did it! You should recognise these new leaves as those of whichever fern you chose to propagate.

14   The baby ferns should be introduced slowly to a dryer environment. While they develop and grow, gradually, over a period of weeks, increase the amount of air that gets to them. First, unfasten the lid of the jar (if still using) or make a hole in the plastic bag. Eventually, your fernlings should be open to the air, at least for a few weeks, before you plant them into their forever home.

15   Once the baby true fern has developed two or three leaves it will have grown a root system and so be ready for potting on. Be very gentle as you do so. The baby ferns are small and delicate, and, after all this work, you must be careful not to kill them by being heavy-handed.

Plant Care

Water	If possible, use rainwater (we microwave it for two minutes to kill any airborne bugs), or boiled water will do (once completely cool). It is recommended to water the soil and not the leaves, to avoid leaf rot. Ferns' natural environment is shady banks and woodland, and cliff edges, so they like to be moist at all times, especially when small.
Food	These slow-growing ferns don't need a huge amount of food, so a half-strength feed every two weeks in spring and early summer will be plenty.
Light	Ferns also like full or partial shade, and no more than three hours a day in full sun. This rules out windowsills, unless they face northeast to northwest in the northern hemisphere (southeast to southwest in the southern).
Note	Ferns are one of the few houseplants that also live naturally in the UK, so they thrive in a temperate climate. Central heating is the enemy, and you may have to relocate the plant to a cool hall or porch as the heat comes on in autumn and winter.

Propagate

Echeveria

Seed propagation

'Succulent' is the name for a group of over 2,000 species of plants that originate in dry climates and have adapted over time to store water in their leaves. Cacti are succulents too, just prickly ones. Succulents such as echeveria are widely available these days in supermarkets, gift shops and florists. They are inexpensive and their geometric leaf patterns are easy on the eye.

Most of the methods in this book have focused on asexual propagation, but this is to overlook the most common and obvious form of regeneration: the germination of seeds. Growing plants from their own seed brings a new level of pleasure. It's satisfying to see something strong and resilient emerge from the tiniest speck.

The following method can be adapted to a number of flowering succulents, but for the purposes of this project we'll focus our attention on the echeveria genus, the topsy-turvy plant (*Echeveria lilacina* 'Ghost echeveria') in particular. These plants tend to flower in the summer, so you'll have to wait until then to begin this project.

You Will Need

- Fine paintbrush
- Gardening scissors or pruning knife
- Plant pot or glass, for drying the flower head
- Brown paper bag and elastic band
- Piece of paper
- Pin or cocktail stick (toothpick)
- Small paper envelope (optional)
- Fine sand
- 10cm (4in)-diameter plant pot
- Perlite mix
- Waterproof tray
- Cling film (plastic wrap)
- Pots and perlite mix, for potting on

How to Propagate
Echeveria

1 — When the time is right for your succulent to flower, you'll notice a tall stalk rising from the mother plant. Let this grow until it produces buds and starts to flower.

2 — When the first few flowers are open, you'll need to pollinate the buds yourself. Use the paintbrush to tickle the inside of each bloom, taking care to move pollen all around the flower.

3 — Now take a clean pair of gardening scissors or a pruning knife and sever each flower stalk at the base. If you don't remove the flower stalk at this point, the succulent will start to divide in two, losing its pleasing shape.

4 — Place the flower stalks (right side up) in an empty plant pot or glass and allow them to dry out.

5 — If the flowers have been fertilised, you should notice the seed pods (at the base of the flower) becoming plump. Over time, they will become dry to the touch, and over several weeks begin to turn a paler colour.

6 — The pods will eventually burst open, so before this happens place the entire stalk in the paper bag. Leave in a dry environment and shake the bag every couple of weeks, peeking inside to see if the pods have shattered and expelled their seeds. Bear in mind that these seeds are extremely small and might appear as a fine dust, so be sure to carefully seal the bag with an elastic band so you don't lose your tiny harvest.

7   Once the seeds have been ejected into the bag, empty the contents on to a clean piece of paper and use a pin or cocktail stick to separate the seeds from the debris. It's a good idea to put the seeds in a small envelope for safe-keeping – one surprise sneeze will ruin your hopes of succulent propagation.

8   It's best to sow the seeds immediately. For ease of sowing, mix the newly gathered seeds with twice the volume of fine sand. This will create a more substantial seed-laden powder that's easier to distribute when planting.

9   Fill the plant pot with perlite mix and tap it gently to settle the mix. Carefully sprinkle the seed-and-sand mix very finely over the soil. If you have a lot of seed mix you can do this with several pots at the same time to maximise your yield.

10   Fill the waterproof tray with 2cm (¾in) of water and stand the filled pots in the water. This will allow each pot to draw up water from the tray, so you don't disturb the fine seed mix by watering from above.

11   Cover the whole tray in cling film and place it in a bright location with a daytime temperature of about 18°C (64°F) – anything above 21°C (70°F) might stop the germination process. Replenish the water when needed, and be on the lookout for signs of fungus (which would show itself as a fine white fur). If you do discover fungus on the surface of the perlite mix this can be treated with fungicide.

12   Within a month or two, tiny leaves should start to appear in the soil. When they do, discard the cling film and remove the pots from the tray. It's time to begin watering the baby plants sparingly (don't let the soil dry out completely).

13   As the plants grow, they should be repotted separately into free-draining containers filled with perlite mix. Select pots that are slightly larger than the circumference of the growing echeveria.

Plant Care

Water	For fully grown plants, let the soil dry out completely between waterings. It's also best to water directly on to the soil rather than on to the plant's leaves. Standing pots in a tray of water for 30 minutes instead of watering from above is a great way to avoid getting water on the leaves.
Food	Just once a year is more than enough.
Light	These plants love the light, so a windowsill is a perfect home. If symmetry is your master, you might want to pay attention to the way the plants stretch towards a light source. You can turn the pots once a week to help retain a circular shape.
Temperature	Most succulents can handle a variety of temperatures (as they do in the desert), but it's best to keep most of them at a moderate room temperature to avoid shocking their systems.
Also try this with	'Sunrise succulent' or 'Sand Rose' (*Anacampseros rufescens*)

Houseplant Evolution

You could say we're only the latest in a long line of dirty boys and girls who've toiled in the fertile soil of Hackney. For hundreds of years the fields – that now lie deep beneath our feet – fed the city, a patchwork of kitchen gardens bursting with food bound for London's bustling markets. But what's perhaps less well known is the role the local area played in how our houseplants and gardens look to this day.

We met up with Danielle Patten, curator at Hackney's very own Museum of the Home (@museumofthehome). She took us on a private tour of the museum, which is arranged as a series of interiors running chronologically from the 1600s through to the 1990s …

How did plants begin their migration from gardens to parlours?

Plants, in the 1600s and earlier, were all used for a purpose, to clean or deodorise, or as medicine, so for example reed-plants were woven into floormats, or rosemary was dried. Houseplants were still years away, but plant parts – flowers, stems and leaves – were being used throughout the home, as well as in medicines and cures. Don't forget that this was the era of the plague, so people were using plants to try and ward off infection. Early interiors were sparse and functional because 'things' like furniture, utensils, anything really, were expensive and so, in stark contrast to today, most people didn't have many possessions. Weirdly, the watering can or 'pot' arrived before the houseplant because it was used to keep the reed floormats flexible and moist, to trap the dust!

When did the more recognisable houseplants come about?

If we move through the rooms from the 1600s and 1700s, it's not until the 1800s and the industrial era that ceramics such as plant pots become more common. Manufacture made decorative objects much more affordable, so it was at this time that plants and flowers started to make their way inside the house, literally because people had something affordable to put them in. At this time local horticultural hero, Conrad Loddiges, was importing seeds from around the world to his heated glasshouses just off Mare Street, East London. But even the cutting-edge, steam-powered technology of the day couldn't solve the problem of how to get living plants to survive the long ocean voyages, and this severely limited what was available.

How did the kind of plants we grow inside change?

Slowly, at first. Loddiges and his sons were importing seeds of some now-familiar plants, such as the ZZ plant (pictured overleaf), but it was very expensive. Then, in the 1830s, another local hero and a friend of the Loddiges, Dr Nathaniel Bagshaw Ward, noticed how, of his struggling collection of ferns, one plant – which had accidentally rooted underneath an upturned glass – thrived. Ward realised both that the poisonous London air was killing his precious fern collection

and that plants could survive hermetically sealed for months at a time. The Wardian Case (terrarium) was born. It meant that, for the first time, delicate propagations could survive months at sea.

This is the 1870 room (see page 151) and you can see the change – it's packed full of plants and flowers.
Yes, and it even has a Wardian Case! That takes pride of place, stuffed with hart's-tongue ferns to reflect the fashionable craze of the day, fern-collecting. With the Wardian case came new plants from the tropics – plants that couldn't survive an English winter outside, so they soon found a new home, inside the home. Interestingly – and we see this in household manuals of the day (a kind of lifestyle guide) – as life became increasingly urban, the Victorians realised the importance of houseplants for our well-being, and not just aesthetics. The exploitation that came with globalisation, the industrial production of pots and stands, the manufacture of sophisticated devices such as terrariums, and increased literacy (meaning people could read about and follow these fashions) intersected in houseplants, feeding their blooming popularity, which remains to this day.

This is evident in the 1990s room – a much more familiar space to us.
Yes, by now the role houseplants play in keeping us happy and healthy was well understood, but the trend was clearly towards plants that are easy to look after. Modern people lead

busy lives, with long commutes, and both partners are likely to work away from home all day. Houseplants need to reflect this relative neglect, to be hardwearing and unkillable. These hardy, easy-to-care-for plants (many of which evolved in desert or mountain environments) have found an entirely new niche – again aided by technology – our centrally heated homes.

In a post-COVID world, with people perhaps increasingly working from home, will houseplants assume ever greater importance?
COVID lockdowns led to a boom in houseplant sales, but it's a trend that already existed. In some ways, houseplants have gone full circle, back to their origins in the seventeenth century. They are here to perform a function, to make us feel better. Perhaps, going forward, we'll use technology to change what we grow inside once more, but such plants will surely have a function – increasingly everything in the home must earn its keep. But, at the same time, as the world grows increasingly urban, so our need to grow houseplants will only build.

Index

Glossary

Cultivar: a type of plant that's been grown through selective breeding.

Growing medium: the general term for what you grow your plants and cuttings in. This could be perlite, a mix of peat-free compost, riddled garden soil or any mix, formulated to a plant's needs.

Hardening-off: if your propagation has been raised in a protected environment, such as a mini-greenhouse, glass jar or plastic bag, then the young plant will need to be hardened-off, which is to slowly remove the protective environment over a period of a few days so that the plant can get used to life away from its nursery.

Node: the point on the stem where the leaves are (or were) attached. It is the site on many plants that is most likely to propagate.

Perlite: bright white type of volcanic glass that has been heated until it 'pops', making it very absorbent. It retains moisture, aids drainage and is great for aerating the soil.

Photosynthesis: the biochemical process by which sunlight is converted into the nutrients needed by a plant to grow and thrive.

Pinching out: the removal of the plant tips or flowers to either remove dying buds and encourage growth or to maintain the shape of the plant.

Potting compost: is a growing medium that is specifically formulated for potting up cuttings.

Potting on: once your propagations are established in the same pot or tray, they'll need to be potted on individually.

Riddled: sieved (the word comes from the round, large-holed garden sieve which is called a riddle).

Suckers: are growths that start at the roots or base of some plants and can be cut away to propagate.

Variegated: some plants have lighter pigmentation along the leaves. This is called variegation and often means they need more light than a non-variegated cultivar.

Vermiculite: Similar to perlite, but vermiculite has slightly greater properties of absorption. Another difference is aesthetic, as vermiculite is brown/gold and perlite is bright white.

Acknowledgements

Thanks to Eve and Chelsea for channelling our ideas into this lovely book.
Special thanks to India for her beautiful photography.
Paul would like to thank Robin for his sandwiches and unrelenting wit.
Robin would like to thank Daniel, whose unwavering support means the world.

About the Authors

Two Dirty Boys
Paul and Robin met randomly on a spooky Halloween night way back
in 2010 – and have been haunting each other's lives ever since. On social
media, they are the Two Dirty Boys, charting their plant successes but also
their (numerous) failures, because they believe the online world needs a bit
of a reality check, not just an endless glossy supply of filtered perfection.
Since taking on an allotment in East London, they've expanded their growing
capabilities beyond fruit and veg to houseplants – all shared with the
wonderfully supportive online 'growing' community.

In 2020, they released their first book *Regrown: How to Grow Fruit, Herbs
and Vegetables from Kitchen Scraps* which has now been translated into
several languages.

Follow them across platforms: @TwoDirtyBoys.

Paul Anderton
Paul grew up in Lytham St Anne's, Lancashire, the son of two teachers. He has
always had an affinity with nature, displaying excessive empathy for discarded
or damaged plants, even as a child. He works in brand partnerships and lives in
Bethnal Green with his border terrier, Willy, and hundreds of houseplants.

Robin Daly
Robin's Devonian grandma instilled in him a love of the natural world. Mrs Daly
would try to propagate from anything she liked the look of, often on the way to
collect her pension, to Robin's total embarrassment. Her home was a veritable
Kew Gardens of scavenged, but thriving, houseplants. Robin admits to still
feeling the thrill of taking a cutting – even after all these years 'it feels naughty.'

Published in 2022 by Hardie Grant Books,
an imprint of Hardie Grant Publishing
Hardie Grant Books (London)
5th & 6th Floors
52–54 Southwark Street
London SE1 1UN

Hardie Grant Books (Melbourne)
Building 1, 658 Church Street
Richmond, Victoria 3121
hardiegrantbooks.com

British Library Cataloguing-in-Publication Data. A catalogue
record for this book is available from the British Library.
Propagate by Paul Anderton and Robin Daly
ISBN: 978-1-78488-492-5

Publisher: Kajal Mistry
Commissioning Editor: Eve Marleau
Senior Editor: Chelsea Edwards
Design: Stuart Hardie
Photography: India Whiley-Morton
Copyeditor: Rosie Fairhead
Proofreader: Jessica Spencer
Indexer: Vanessa Bird
Colour Reproduction by p2d
Printed and bound in China
by Leo Paper Products Ltd

10 9 8 7 6 5 4 3 2 1

MIX
Paper from
responsible sources
FSC
www.fsc.org
FSC™ C020056